YOUR ATTITUDE IS SHOWING

A Primer on Human Relations

third edition

Elwood N. Chapman

Chaffey College, Alta Loma, California

SCIENCE RESEARCH ASSOCIATES, INC.

Chicago, Palo Alto, Toronto, Henley-on-Thames, Sydney, Paris, Stuttgart

A Subsidiary of IBM

Information for ordering this book and *Supervisor's Survival Kit* (companion book) may be obtained from:

Science Research Associates, Inc.
College Division
1540 Page Mill Road
Palo Alto, California 94304

Library of Congress Cataloging in Publication Data

Chapman, Elwood N.
   Your attitude is showing

   1. Psychology, Industrial.   2. Industrial sociology.
I. Title.
HF5548.8.C36   1977   158.7   77-14526
ISBN 0-574-20575-6

Publisher's Preface

A few years ago, SRA published the first edition of *Your Attitude Is Showing*. Now one quarter of a million copies later, the third edition of this book is appearing. What accounts for the extraordinary success of this small book? I believe it is a recognition on the part of the buyer that simple, yet sound ideas do not go out of date. If anything, in today's complex world a person's attitude is more important than ever.

Your Attitude Is Showing has stood the test of time, and we believe this third edition will be more successful than ever. All of us at SRA would like to thank Elwood Chapman for his consistently positive attitude over the years. I'm convinced that Chap's attitude contributed greatly to the success of this book. What better evidence that in the final analysis—attitude does make a difference.

Michael G. Crisp
Vice President and
College Publisher

Contents

Case Problems

Preface

The first two editions of *Your Attitude Is Showing* have been used as a classroom text by teachers and work-experience coordinators in a wide variety of educational institutions. The book has also been heavily purchased by businesses and by organizations (especially hospitals) as an important training tool for both new and experienced employees and supervisors. In addition, it has found its way into many personal libraries. Today, more than ever, it is recognized as a basic primer in the field of business human relations.

Your Attitude Is Showing is a positive book. It has helped individuals of all ages and backgrounds play their human-relations roles with greater understanding and sensitivity. The book has been especially helpful to young people faced with the problem of bridging the gap between campus and career. It has prepared them to cope with many human and business problems, including the crucial first-job interview.

I believe this third edition will be equally welcomed by teachers and students, managers and employees. I based my revisions upon research and consultation with the people who used the previous editions most extensively. I have added many new features to meet contemporary needs. These include a new chapter on self-motivation, more current and sophisticated case problems, and greater emphasis on the communication of "attitude" during the job-finding process.

As you read and study *Your Attitude Is Showing*, keep in mind that people who develop skills in human relations find greater on-the-job happiness, contribute more to the success of their organizations, and often advance more quickly into supervisory and managerial positions.

Introduction

This book could be appropriately subtitled *Gaining Personal Success in Business*, for nothing has more impact on career success than one's attitude. Illustrations like the one below will help you become more aware of this—and enjoy the book as well. Each drawing shows an amoeba—the microscopic, one-celled creature that is constantly changing in size and shape, and is often referred to as the lowest form of life. I hope the little amoeba will act as a reminder to you that, no matter where you are or what you are doing, *Your Attitude Is Showing*.

"After all, I'm just an amoeba."

1

You Can't Escape Human Relations

Most employees greatly underestimate the importance of human relations in building their careers.

They pass it off as nothing more than common sense.

They say it is something one handles intuitively.

They claim it is something that is automatically taken care of when it happens, so why worry about it in advance?

But what exactly is involved in human relations?

Part of human relations is being sociable, courteous, and adaptable. It is smiling. It is keeping out of trouble with fellow workers. It is following the rules of simple etiquette. It is good taste. But as important as these characteristics are to personal success, they are not enough. Human relations is much more than just getting people to like you.

"I've heard all that old stuff before."

Human relations is also knowing how to handle difficult problems when they arise. It is learning to work well under demanding and sometimes unfair superiors. It is understanding yourself and others. It is building sound working relationships in controversial situations. It is knowing how to restore a working relationship that has deteriorated. It is learning to live with your frustrations without hurting others or jeopardizing your own career. It is communicating a positive attitude during an interview. In short, it is building and maintaining relationships in many directions, with many different kinds of people.

In the business world, human relations is viewed best in terms of productivity.

Productivity!

Ah, there is a word worth knowing about. Why? Because that word is the key to your future and the future of the organization you have joined.

Of course, good human relations cannot substitute for work. It cannot camouflage a sloppy performance. Employees are valued primarily for the amount of work they turn out. Your employer will expect you to do your share of the work load—and if you are interested in moving ahead, you will want to do more than your share. An employer will not be interested for long in an employee who has a great attitude but produces very little.

But getting the work out is only one side of the coin. You should accomplish this work and still be sensitive to the needs of those who work with you. You should perform your work without trying to show up your fellow workers or antagonize them. You should carry your full load in such a way that others will be encouraged to follow you rather than reject you.

No matter how ambitious or capable you are, you cannot become the kind of employee you want to be (or the kind of employee management wants you to be) without learning how to work effectively with people. It would be career suicide to join an organization and ignore the people who work around you. You simply cannot escape human relations.

Does this mean that you should deliberately set out to play a game of human relations on your new job? The answer depends upon what you mean by "playing a game."

If you mean that you should play up to those who can do you the most good and pay little attention to the others, the answer is, of course, no.

If you mean that you should devise a master strategy which will give you the breaks at the expense of other people, the answer is again no.

If, however, you mean that you should sincerely do everything you can to build strong, friendly, and honest working relationships with *all* the people you work with—fellow employees and supervisors alike—the answer is an unqualified yes.

Does this come as a shock?

If so, think about it. Working hard is not enough in our modern society. It may have been 30 years ago, but it isn't today. You, as a new employee, have a definite human relations duty.

You can't ignore it.

You can't postpone it.

From the moment you join an organization you assume two responsibilities: (1) to do a job—the *best* job you can do with the work assigned to you, and (2) to get along with *all* people to the best of your ability. It is the right combination of these two factors that spells success.

Perhaps you will graduate from high school or a community college soon and your first full-time job will be with a large service company. Or maybe you will complete a four-year college course with a degree in engineering or business administration and elect to join a large industrial corporation. Then again, perhaps you are a reentry person attending an educational institution to prepare for a career after several years' absence from the labor market. Or perhaps after working a number of years for a particular company, you have decided to change jobs to make a fresh start.

The possibilities are endless, but no matter what your personal conditions are now or what they may be in the future, your first full-time job will give you your big chance. Whether you start out as a stock girl in a department store, a member of a research team for a government bureau, or a starting supervisor, it is likely that you will receive some useful training as you get started on the job. This is true because you were not employed so much for what you already know as for what you can learn in the future. You were hired for your potential, and the company that is employing you wants to help you realize that potential.

It would be wrong, of course, to say that the skills or abilities you possess are unimportant. To be sure, if you are employed as a secretary, your skill at taking shorthand is important. If you are employed as an apprentice machinist, your mathematical ability is important. If you are a college graduate in a management-trainee program, your general background in business administration or marketing is important. These skills helped you win your present position and they will help you make progress.

But they are not enough.

In order to make your education and experience work for you properly, you must become competent in human relations. You must develop in a different setting. You must learn the technique of working with others.

Why?

Because your behavior has a direct bearing on the efficiency of others. Because your contribution will not always be an individual contribution; it will often be a group effort, and you will only be a part of the group. Because what you accomplish will be in direct proportion to how well you get along with the people who work with you, above you, or for you.

Almost everything you do will have an effect on other people. If the effect is good, people may do a better job. If the effect is bad, they may be less productive. Your *personal* work effort will not be enough. You should conduct yourself in such a manner that those who work with you and near you will also become more effective.

Now let's take a closer look at this word *productivity*. Productivity is a significant word in business, industry, and government today. Every organization is operated either to make a profit or to reach a certain level of productivity.

Management has its own ways of measuring work productivity. Some jobs are more easily measured than others. If you are employed as a factory worker, for example, your productivity would be measured by the amount of work you perform over a certain time.

Some organizations employ time-study people to measure the time required to perform a given task, and to establish standards of performance. As an employee of such a company you would be expected to exceed this standard. If you are employed in a sales organization, for instance, you might be given a sales quota that you would be expected to reach or exceed.

The point is that everyone's productivity is measured. We must all live up to the standards that prevail in our particular business. There is some form of measurement or evaluation for every job.

However, our value is measured not only by the actual work we do, but also by the *contribution* we make to the department as a whole. This is human relations—as management sees it. Productivity is not only an individual matter; it is also a divisional or departmental matter. For management has discovered that the way in which people get along together has a great deal to do with departmental productivity.

For example, let us assume you started out as a meter reader for an electric utility. One would at first assume that your productivity would be measured by the number of meters you could read correctly in a given time. This is basically true, but it doesn't stop at that point. There is the matter of how you get along with homeowners and customers and, even more important, how your supervisor and the other employees react to you.

In other words, a meter reader is never just a meter reader. He (or she) is a member of a team. He is a potential supervisor. He is a potential manager. He is also a potential drawback to the company if he doesn't handle things properly. And as far as his advancement is concerned, his human-relations ability may be as important as his job performance—providing, of course, that he is above average in this respect.

Let us take the example of a checker in a supermarket. The productivity of a checker is usually measured in three ways: speed, accuracy, and relations with customers. But it doesn't stop there. Why? Because the way others react to her (or him) has an influence on *their* productivity as well as on the productivity of the checker herself. If she is an excellent checker and measures above others in all three categories, one would think she would be the best checker of all. But would she be? Not necessarily.

Let us assume that it is a peak period in the supermarket and all checkers are extremely busy. Shoppers are lined up in front of each check stand. One of the other checkers suddenly runs out of paper sacks and calls for our "superior" checker to toss him a few. What if our checker says, "Come and get 'em if you want 'em." What would happen? A psychological barrier would immediately arise between the two checkers. The checker requesting the bags would be embarrassed in front of the customers and as a result, his speed, accuracy, and relations with customers would deteriorate. So even though our superior checker is superior in all three categories, she has hurt the total productivity of the operation. Nobody can beat her as far as doing her assigned job is concerned. However, she has failed to live up to good human-relations standards.

A third example might be a teller in a bank. Suppose a young woman is fast, accurate, and effective with customers. In fact, she is so good that she attracts more customers to her window than the other tellers and as a result carries a very high work load in comparison with the others. However, our teller has a haughty attitude. She doesn't mix with the others. Consequently, the other tellers build up resentment toward her, and their productivity is lowered. In this example it is conceivable that the young teller actually hurts the efficiency of the department even though her personal productivity is the *highest*.

In other words, productivity is not only what you do yourself; it is also the influence, good or bad, you have on others. You not only have a job to perform, you have a contribution to make to your fellow employees. It is not a contribution that always comes easy. On occasion you may find it necessary to work effectively with someone you do not like. If you succeed, you have accepted a difficult challenge and you have made a worthwhile contribution. If you fail, at least try to learn something from the experience and wait for another chance, for it is a contribution that you should eventually make. The worker who keeps his or her personal productivity high and at the same time is sensitive enough to have a beneficial influence on others is the worker management will probably reward.

Human relations knows no age or experience level. You may be a recent high school or college graduate starting your first job, a middle-aged widow entering the labor market for the first time, a senior citizen taking up a new career, a housewife returning to a job she left years ago, or a long-time career employee only a few years from retirement—whatever your situation is, human relations will play a vital role in the years that lie ahead.

Once you understand that there is no escape from human relations, you will be in a position to deal with it and to receive the greatest compliment of all—to be recognized, perhaps by a supervisor or a fellow employee, as having concern for others. Your knowledge about human relations will have earned you that distinction.

PROBLEM 1
Reality

Rod was very pleased with himself when he, along with two other equally qualified people, won a job with the Southern Electrical Company.

After successfully completing his three-month probationary period, Rod was assigned to a department that was known for its high productivity and outstanding teamwork. Rod's supervisor told him how lucky he was to win the assignment and then quietly suggested that he make a special effort to get along with everybody.

Rod worked hard and efficiently in his new assignment, but he made a series of human-relations mistakes. For example, he was rather impatient with one co-worker who was late in returning some equipment. Another time he complained that his lunch period was delayed because he had to wait for a fellow employee to return. On still another occasion he was openly upset when his work load was temporarily increased one day because a co-worker had to go home sick.

After a few weeks had passed, the supervisor called Rod into his office and had a second, more serious talk with him. At the end of the interview, Rod asked if his work was satisfactory. The supervisor told him it was substantially above average but that his human-relations skills could show some improvement.

Some months later Rod heard that the two people who were hired at the same time he was had received promotions. He passed it off by saying, "In this outfit it isn't what you know but who you know that counts."

Was Rod justified in feeling this way? What else might Rod's supervisor have done to help him with his problem? (For a suggested answer, see page 186.)

2

Human Relations
Can Make or Break You

Now that you have read the first chapter, perhaps you have a few questions you would like to ask. Let us create a third party, called Joe Harvey, to ask a series of questions for you.

I am a rather quiet and timid person. Does this mean that I must work harder than others to be good at human relations?

It may. Many people who are oversensitive about being friendly and communicating with new acquaintances need to make a special effort at the beginning. It is difficult to build good relationships with strangers if you withdraw and refuse to give them a chance to know you.

People who are very quiet or self-sufficient sometimes forget that their silence may be interpreted as aloofness, indifference, or even hostility. To avoid misinterpretation you should learn

"Don't ask me . . . I just work here."

to communicate frequently and openly with the people you work with. However, Joe, it should be encouraging for you to know that many withdrawn people become highly skilled at human relations later on. The very sensitivity that caused them to withdraw in the first place helps them to be more aware of others' needs.

I am 22 and am planning to join a large, conservative organization. How much of a handicap is my youth?

If you can learn to create and maintain good relationships with all people, including those much older than yourself, age need not be a handicap at all. One way to do this is to respect older people's experience and to learn as much as possible from them. The building of such relationships will test your human-relations skills.

This is a tough question, but how can I gain greater inner confidence so that I can approach people and start building good working relationships with them?

Sometimes you should gamble and take the first step instead of standing on the sidelines thinking about it. This means that you should greet your fellow workers pleasantly even though they might ignore you from time to time. It means that you should talk with people even though you feel clumsy about it and feel that what you say might be rejected. Of course, taking such initiative can often be unsettling. However, with experience you will sense a new inner confidence that will make it much easier for you in the future.

Will paying more attention to human relations give me a brighter future?

Your question deserves an unqualified yes answer, Joe. Management experts in general agree that those employees who concentrate on good human relations get the best jobs and eventually rise to the top in most organizations. Those who pay little attention to human relations seem to get lost and are pushed into the least desirable jobs. All organizations are built around people, and when you build healthy relationships with your fellow workers and supervisors, you open doors that would otherwise be closed.

Look at it this way, Joe: You have a good education; you have a high potential; you have the desire to succeed. All of this is great, but you can't put it to work unless you work well with people—because people, if they want to, can put up road blocks at every corner. Whether you accept it or not, people will control your job future, and the better the relationships you build with them the better things will be for you.

How much human-relations skill must I have to move ahead quickly?

The more the better, of course, but not as much as you might suspect. It is surprising how many capable people ignore the importance of human relations—making it easier, of course, for those who don't. Only a few people actually take the time to think seriously about human relations. You could be different. By reading this book you are concentrating on the problem. You are taking time to study the subject and become more knowledgeable about it. Your efforts should help you become more satisfied with your job and move ahead more quickly.

Why is human relations more important to the worker today than it was thirty or forty years ago?

There are many reasons. Here are six of the most important ones:

1. Business, industrial, and governmental organizations are larger and more complex. Consequently they are more dependent on *group* effort than they were forty years ago. In the old days, more employees worked in isolated jobs than they do today. More interpersonal relationships are necessary in a modern business enterprise.

2. Today more workers are employed in service occupations. Customer relations are an important part of most business organizations, because the future of the organization depends on how well the customer is served. This makes human relations more important throughout the company.

3. There are fewer unskilled jobs in our society today. Years ago people were hired to do routine work that is today done by

machines. They did the isolated specific task and had little to say. There are very few of those jobs left. Most have been replaced by jobs involving close association with other workers. This, in turn, requires more communication.

4. Greater productivity is the key to greater profit and an increase in the standard of living for all people. In order to gain greater productivity for themselves and for co-workers closely associated with them, people need greater competence in human-relations skills.

5. More and more supervisors are being trained in human relations. Because of this, many are more sensitive to the behavior of those working for them. This can cause the supervisor to set higher human-relations standards for all employees.

6. Today's work force is composed of a more varied mix of personalities and cultures than it was forty years ago. Thus the challenge of building better relations with all kinds of people is greater.

Is human relations as important in small organizations as it is in large ones?

Generally speaking, yes. There are some important differences, though between functioning in large and small organizations. Your progress, over a long period, may depend more on good human relations in a large company than in a small company. This is true because there is more supervision and more human-relations responsibility in a large company. Some higher positions in these organizations are almost exclusively leadership positions. In these positions human relations is 60 or 70 percent of the total job.

Remember, too, that most people—some estimate as high as 70 percent—seek careers with large companies. At the same time, these large companies are getting even larger. Of course, it is important to note that there are still excellent opportunities with organizations of a hundred employees or less.

Also, the big companies were the first to introduce human-relations training for supervisors. They are likely to place more importance on it. It follows that because smaller companies may not provide as much training and assistance, you may have to develop human-relations skills on your own.

Will becoming competent in human relations help me become a supervisor sooner?

Emphatically, yes. The degree to which you develop your human-relations skills will strongly influence your progress toward a more responsible position. Of course, other factors, such as your mental ability and your willingness to work, also play an important role. But the daily application of the tips and techniques you learn through this book will unquestionably help you. In short, employees who do not become human-relations competent rarely reach a position of leadership.

I have a friend who is already a supervisor. How can this book help her?

It will help her review and assess the basic human-relations principles and standards that are applicable to those in management roles. You could also suggest the book *Supervisor's Survival Kit* (also published by SRA), which is a companion book to *Your Attitude Is Showing* and a logical follow-up to it.

Must I have high mental ability to become human-relations competent?

No! You may have high mental ability (in terms of IQ) and still not be skillful at human relations. There appears to be little or no correlation between high mental ability and the ability to work well with people. In fact, some individuals with very high mental ability appear to be particularly incompetent in human relations. People and the way they react are not always important to these individuals. They often do not want to be bothered. They can be wonderful research people, but sometimes they are poor supervisors.

Does a person have to be an extrovert to be good at human relations?

No. Extroverts are people who are outgoing and like to be around other people. This can certainly be a plus. Conversely, many people who are quiet and withdrawn can be very smart in dealing with others.

Human relations is *sensitivity* to others. However, extroverted people are often too concerned with themselves to be good at building relations with others. The skills and principles outlined in this book can be learned and applied by both extroverts and introverts.

Why are some people so obviously awkward at human relations?

That's a tough question, Joe, because each personality is different and there could be many complex reasons. Here are a few possibilities. Some individuals are so self-centered that they think only of themselves and therefore give little consideration to the feelings of others. Some are blinded by ambition to the point where they seriously jeopardize their relationships with others. Still others let their emotions spill over at the wrong time, destroying relationships they have carefully built in the past. It may be hard to admit, but we all make mistakes in building and maintaining relationships with people. None of us will ever be perfect, but we should never stop trying to improve.

Does high performance in school guarantee high performance on the job?

No. An individual can be outstanding academically, but be very weak in actual performance on the job. The work environment is different, people are different, and the objectives in business are different from those in the classroom. It is frequently true that a student who is average in the classroom is outstanding on the job, and vice versa. This can mean that some students who are high achievers academically might have more of an adjustment to make to the world of work than those who get more practical experience along the way.

Will I have to change my personality to become better at human relationships?

I doubt if that will be necessary. You are what you are, and you cannot become someone else. However, you can change many of your habits, attitudes, and behavior in working with people. You can develop the personality you already have by using better human relations.

Will this book really help me become human-relations competent?

If you give it a try, yes. But first you must accept these ideas as sound and in keeping with your sense of dignity. Your biggest job, of course, will be to apply what you learn in this book on your present job. If you put an idea or technique into practice long enough, it becomes a habit and you do it automatically. It won't be easy, though, and as I said before, no one is ever human-relations perfect. Your goal is not to become perfect but to become substantially better. This will make the difference you need to become successful.

Will reading this book help me get a job?

Employers are more interested in the human-relations skills of people they hire than ever before. If you can show an interviewer that you are human-relations competent and that your attitude is positive, your chances of landing a job will be far greater.

Human behavior does not change easily. Modification of attitudes and habits is a slow, difficult process. Whether you make these changes will depend on how badly you wish to succeed. This book tells you how to become skillful at human relations.

The rest is up to you.

PROBLEM 2
Adjustment

Ann and George were both young, aggressive, and competent. They joined the M.K. company on the same day and went through the same training program in preparation for identical jobs involving a great deal of close contact with fellow employees.

Although it was not easy, Ann made a good adjustment to her work environment. She was able to do this because of her warm, flexible personality and the application of the human-relations skills she had learned and developed in college. George, on the other hand, made little progress. He appeared rigid and distant to those who worked around him. To a few older and experienced employees he even seemed aloof and hostile. George's supervisor, watching him from a distance, felt he was waiting around expecting others to approach him and be friendly. He seemed to be standing on the sidelines, unable or unwilling to meet people halfway. Perhaps he did not know how to communicate with others.

A few weeks later, during lunch, George told Ann he was going to look for another job. His reasons were as follows: (1) he felt some co-workers were unfriendly, (2) he resented some of his fellow employees, who seemed excessively critical to him, and (3) he felt his supervisor was trying to push him into a mold of conformity that was simply not his style. Why should he go all out in adjusting? After all, building working relationships is a two-way thing. He felt confident that he could find another company that would appreciate him more and give him all the freedom he needed to be himself.

What chance do you think George had of finding a job environment that would make him completely happy? How might his supervisor have helped him in making the adjustment? (For a suggested answer, see page 187.)

3

Hold on to Your Positive Attitude

Attitude is a very common word. You hear it almost every day. Parents talk about it at home. Teachers use it in classes. Supervisors discuss it at work. No other word will have more impact on your future. This is true because your positive attitude is your most priceless personal possession.

If you can create and keep a positive attitude toward your job, your company, and life in general, you should not only move up the ladder of success quickly and gracefully, but you should also be a happier person. If you are unable to do this, you may find many doors closed to you on the job, and your personal life less than exciting.

There are three forms of communication between people. One is the written form—letters, memos, telegrams. The second is

"I'll keep my positive attitude."

the verbal form—face-to-face conversations, telephone conversations, intercom discussions.

These forms of communication are so important to the operation of an organization that we tend to think they are the only ones. We forget that something psychologically very important takes place between people even without the written or spoken word: We transmit our attitudes through facial expressions, hand gestures, and other more subtle forms of body language. So every time you report for work, every time you attend a staff meeting, every time you take a coffee break, and every time you go out socially, be aware that *your attitude is showing.*

Because attitude can play such an important role in your future, let's take a close look at the meaning of the word itself.

Attitude is defined by most psychologists as a mental set that will cause you to respond in a characteristic manner to a given stimulus. A more sophisticated definition is given by G. W. Allport, a prominent social psychologist, in *The Nature of Personality: Selected Papers* (Cambridge, Mass., 1950), p. 13:

> An attitude is a mental and neural state of readiness, organized through experience, exerting a directive and dynamic influence upon the individual's response to all objects and situations with which it is related.

You have, in effect, many attitudes or mental sets in your mind. You have your favorite colors. If red is your favorite color, you have a favorable attitude toward things that are red. If green is not attractive to you, we might say you have a mental set against things that are green. You have attitudes toward certain makes of automobiles, toward certain social institutions (schools, churches, and the like, toward careers, life styles, people, and so on.

The important thing as far as this book is concerned is to realize that you will develop attitudes on your new job. You will build attitudes toward your supervisor and the people you work with, toward the job you do, toward company policies, toward the amount of money you are being paid. In addition to these specific attitudes, you will also have a basic, or total, attitude toward your job and, in a larger sense, toward life itself. Strictly speaking, in this larger sense, attitude is the *way you look at your whole environment.*

You can look at your job in any way you wish. On the one hand, you can focus your attention on all its negative aspects (odd hours, close supervision, poor location). On the other hand, you can focus your attention on the more positive factors of the job (harmonious work environment, good learning opportunities, good benefits). All jobs have both positive and negative factors. How you choose to perceive yours is an important decision.

Attitude is the way you view and interpret your environment. Some people can push the unpleasant things out of their sight and dwell largely on the positive factors. Others seem to enjoy the unpleasant and dwell on these negative factors.

What you see in life influences your attitude.

If you go around looking for what is wrong with things, wondering why things are not better, and complaining about them, then you will be a negative person in the minds of most people. If you do the opposite—look for what is good and don't focus on unpleasant things—you will be a positive person in the minds of most people.

Every job has certain unfavorable or negative things about it. There is no perfect job or position. One job may have more favorable things about it than another, but all jobs have *some* unpleasant things. The employee who dwells on the unfavorable factors has a negative attitude. If he (or she) forces himself to look for factors that are favorable, he will slowly become a more positive person.

If you start your new job with a positive attitude, our concern then is whether it will remain positive. It is possible that you will meet a few people on your work assignment who have negative attitudes and will attempt to persuade you to think as they do. And no doubt you will find a few factors about the job itself that are indeed negative.

To be a positive person, you need not think your company is perfect. This would be foolish. You would eventually become disillusioned. On the other hand, unless you feel that the majority of factors are favorable, you will eventually become negative, and you will show it.

There is another way to look at it. Once you focus your attention more on the negative factors than on the positive, you are hurting yourself and your chances in the future.

The moment you can no longer be positive about your career with your company, your chances for success diminish.

No one can be positive all the time. You will naturally have periods of doubt. These temporary periods of evaluation will not hurt you seriously. But a day-to-day negative attitude that persists over weeks and months will destroy your future with the company. If this should happen, and you honestly feel such an attitude is justified, you should resign.

A positive attitude is essential to career success for many reasons.

1. When you are positive you are usually more energetic, highly motivated, productive, and alert. Thinking about negative things too much has a way of draining your energy. Put another way, a positive attitude opens a gate and lets your inner enthusiasm spill out. A negative attitude, on the other hand, will keep the gate closed.

2. First impressions are important on the job because they often have a lasting effect. People you meet for the first time appear to have little radar sets tuned in to your attitude. If your attitude is positive, they receive a friendly, warm signal, and they are attracted to you. If your attitude is negative, they receive an unfriendly signal, and they try to avoid you.

3. A positive employee contributes to the productivity of others. A negative employee does not. Attitudes are caught more than they are taught! Both negative and positive attitudes are transmitted on the job. They are picked up by others. A persistently negative attitude, like the rotten apple in the barrel, can spoil the positive attitudes of others. It is very difficult to maintain a high level of productivity while working next to a person with a negative attitude.

4. People like you when you are positive. They like to be around you, because you are fun. This makes your job more interesting and exciting, because you are in the middle of things and not on the outside complaining. When you are negative, people prefer to stay clear of you. A negative person may build good relationships with a few other people (who are perhaps negative themselves), but such a person cannot build good relationships with the majority of employees.

5. The kind of attitude you transmit to management will have a great deal to do with your future success. Management con-

stantly reads your mental attitude, even though you may feel you are successful in covering it up. Supervisors can determine your attitude by how you approach your job, react to directives, handle problems, and work with others. If you are positive you will be given greater consideration when special assignments and promotional opportunities arise.

It is important to realize that a positive attitude is far more than a smile. A smile, of course, is helpful in transmitting an inner positive attitude. However, some people transmit a positive attitude even though they seldom smile. They do this by the positive way they treat others, the way they look at their responsibilities, and the perspective they take when faced with a problem.

Attitude is a highly personal thing. It is very close to your ego, to the way you look at yourself. Because of this, attitude is not easy to talk about. People often freeze when the word is mentioned. As a result, management may never talk to you about your attitude. They may never say to an employee, "Joe, let's be honest. Your attitude is negative. What are you going to do about it?" *But everyone will know when it is showing.*

How, then, do you make sure you keep your positive attitude when things get tough? How do you keep a good grip on it when you are discouraged? How do you keep it in good repair on a day-to-day basis over the years? Here are a few simple suggestions.

1. *Build a more positive attitude in one environment and you will be more successful in another.* Your positive or negative attitude is not something that you can hang on a hook. It follows you wherever you go. It is reasonable to assume then that if you make a greater effort to be a more positive person in your social and personal life, this will automatically spill over and help you on the job. By the same token, if you make a greater effort to develop a more positive attitude at work, this will in turn make a contribution to your social and personal life. One effort will complement the other.

2. *Talk about positive things.* Negative comments are seldom welcomed by fellow workers on the job; nor are they welcomed by those you meet in the social scene. The solution? Be complimentary. Constant gripers and complainers seldom build healthy and exciting relationships with others.

3. *Look for the good things in the people you work with, especially your supervisors.* Nobody is perfect, but almost everybody has a few worthwhile qualities. If you dwell on people's good features it will be easier for you to like them and easier for them to like you. Make no mistake about one thing: people usually know how you react to them even if you don't communicate verbally.

4. *Look for the good things in your department.* What are the factors that make it a good place to work? Do you like the hours, the physical environment, the people, the actual work you are doing, the atmosphere? Of course, you are not expected to like everything. No department or work assignment is perfect. But if you concentrate on the good things, the negative factors may seem less important and will not bother you as much. This does not mean that you should ignore negative elements that should be changed. Far from it! A positive person is not a weak person. A positive person is usually confident, assertive, and an "agent of change" within an organization. You are not expected to submit to all factors in your work environment. Management is not seeking passive people who meekly conform. They want spirited, positive people who will make improvements.

5. *Look for the good things in your company.* Just as there are no perfect departments, there are no perfect companies. Nevertheless, almost all organizations have many good features. Is your company progressive? What about opportunities for promotion? Do you have chances for self-improvement? What about your wage and benefit package? Do you have the freedom you seek? You cannot expect to have everything you would like, but there should be enough to keep you positive. If there isn't, you should look elsewhere.

If you decide to stay with a company for a long time, you would be wise to concentrate on its good features. This may take a great amount of personal fortitude on your part but it is the best way to keep your career on an upward track. If you think positively, you will act positively and you will succeed.

6. *Don't permit a fellow worker (or even a supervisor) who has a negative attitude to trap you into his (or her) way of thinking.* You may not be able to change his attitude, but at least you can protect your own positive attitude from becoming negative. The story of Sandy will emphasize this point.

Sandy was a little uneasy about starting her new job. It was a fine opportunity and she knew the standards were very high. Would she have the skills needed? Could she learn fast enough to please her supervisor? Would the older employees like her? Although Sandy's concern was understandable, it was not justified. In addition to being highly qualified for the job, she also had a happy, positive attitude that wouldn't stop. She was seldom depressed.

Everything went very well for Sandy for a while. Her positive attitude was appreciated by all. Slowly, however, her fellow workers and supervisor noticed a change. She became more critical of her colleagues, her job, and the company. Her usual friendly greetings and helpful ideas were gradually replaced by complaints. What had happened? Without realizing it, Sandy was showing the effects of the friendships she had made on the job. Needing acceptance in a strange environment, she had welcomed the attention of a clique of employees who had a negative attitude —a group that management already viewed critically.

Sandy was not able to confine her negative attitude to her job. Soon, again without realizing it, she let her negative attitude spill over into her social life. In fact, it troubled her boyfriend so much that he had it out with her one night. His words were a little rough. "Look, Sandy. When you are happy you are very attractive and fun to be around. But frankly, when you are negative, you are a real bore and I never have a good time with you. I think those so-called friends you hang around with on the job are killing what was once a beautiful personality."

It wasn't a happy evening, but Sandy got the message. She made a vow to recapture and hang on to the positive attitude she had previously enjoyed. Not only was she successful in doing this but she also converted a few of her previously negative friends to her way of thinking. Her action saved her career with the company.

It is only realistic to recognize that a positive attitude is not a cure-all for every kind of behavior problem. But it is important to continue to evaluate one's attitude. Perhaps the best way to do this is to be aware of the acceptance or nonacceptance of the people around you.

One of the most critical "attitude communication" periods an individual faces is during a job interview. In this situation the interviewer is often attempting to discover the attitude of the applicant to supplement the hard data found on the application form or résumé. It is during such periods that one often becomes aware that attitude is transmitted through grooming, facial reactions, body language, and other nonverbal signals.

The following little saying may help you hold on to your positive attitude. You may wish to copy it down on a small card and use it as a reminder. If you read it over and over, you will understand what we have been talking about in this chapter.

YOUR ATTITUDE SPEAKS SO LOUDLY I
CAN'T HEAR WHAT YOU HAVE TO SAY.

PROBLEM 3
Attitude

Manuel was an art major in high school and college. He was a highly sensitive individual with considerable talent. His art teachers constantly praised his work, and he won a number of prizes in campus art shows.

Upon graduating from his community college, he made many attempts to find a job in commercial art. No luck. After many disappointments, he reluctantly accepted a position with a large retail chain that would only have limited use for his talent in the area of merchandising display.

Manuel decided to make the most of his situation and began his career with a positive attitude. He quickly demonstrated that he had both talent and managerial ability. His future looked bright. He was happy.

Some time later, however, Manuel's supervisor noticed a definite change in his attitude. Manuel's enthusiasm started to dwindle. He began giving excuses for not getting things done. His displays were not up to standard. His relationships with people began to deteriorate.

The manager had two heart-to-heart talks with Manuel, but no reason could be pinpointed other than the general assumption that he might be more positive in a job where he could make better use of his creative talents. At any rate a change in attitude and productivity was not forthcoming. This continued for over a year. One day, after a long, upsetting talk with his supervisor, Manuel gave two weeks' notice. That night, over a few beers, he said to one of his close friends, "I should have resigned a year ago—on the very day I noticed my attitude changing. I have been in a job all this time where it has been impossible to be positive."

Is it possible for a person to know the exact day or week his attitude changes? Did Manuel help or hurt himself by staying on the job even though his attitude and productivity deteriorated? Do many people, forced to take a secondary career choice, hurt their future through the negative attitudes they show because they are unable to adjust? (For a suggested answer, see page 188.)

Vertical and Horizontal Working Relationships

When you meet a supervisor or fellow worker for the first time, a psychological reaction takes place: each person instantaneously interprets the other. It is a feeling you can't define. You know something is happening, but you can't put your finger on it. Slowly, as you and the other individual see each other more frequently and get to know each other better, these initial feelings mature into what is called a *relationship*.

A relationship is a *feeling thing* that exists between two people who associate with each other. You can't see, hear, taste, smell, or touch a relationship—you can only feel it in a psychological sense. Relationships that exist on the job are usually different from those you build in the social scene. They are relationships that exist only because you selected a certain company and were assigned to work with certain people in a specific department. In other words, in your social life you have a choice; on the job you do not. Neverthe-

"Relationships are that important?"

less, working relationships are extremely important to you and your future because they will have a strong influence on your personality and personal productivity, as well as on that of others.

Working relationships of this nature are fascinating to study. For example, one interesting characteristic is that two persons cannot meet regularly on the job or work in the same general areas *without* having a relationship. So the first thing to learn about working relationships is that whether you like it or not, one will exist between you and every employee or supervisor with whom you have regular contact.

You need not work next to this person.

You need not speak to her (or him).

You need not even have a desire to know her.

Yet, a relationship will exist. There appears to be no way to neutralize a relationship under these conditions. The very fact that you might decide to ignore a person does not destroy the relationship; in fact, the opposite may happen. The relationship may become more tense and psychologically powerful. Let us take a specific example.

You notice an employee working in a department next to you. In an attempt to be friendly, you say hello in a very pleasant way to this person the first day on the job, and you receive no reply.

Does this mean the relationship is cut off at this point?

Far from it! You may feel that her failure to reply is a slight to you, and this may naturally disturb you. You may decide not to take the initiative again. Nevertheless, you will remember this person clearly and wonder what will happen in the future.

The person to whom you said hello, on the other hand, has had some kind of reaction to your friendly gesture. She may feel that she treated you in an unfriendly manner (perhaps she was not feeling well that day), and might welcome another opportunity to be more friendly. Or, she may have interpreted your hello as being a little too forward on your part as a new employee and decided to be cool toward you.

You could ignore her. You could avoid verbal contact. You and she could see each other only a few times each week.

Would a relationship exist?

Yes, indeed. Two persons have made contact with each other. They see each other occasionally. They work for the same company. As long as these factors exist, a relationship must exist. Under these conditions you cannot erase a relationship. The attempt on the part of one person to withdraw serves only to make the relationship more emotionally charged; it does not in any manner eliminate it.

You cannot consistently work with or near people or communicate with them frequently without having working relationships with them.

There is another interesting characteristic about these relationships when viewed objectively. They are either strong or weak, warm or cool, healthy or unhealthy, friendly or distant. There appears to be no absolute neutral ground. Every relationship has a very small positive or negative content.

Have you ever heard someone say, "I can take her or leave her"? The phrase usually means that it doesn't make any difference whether the person referred to is around or not. But the very fact that one makes such a comment indicates that it would be better if the person were not around. The relationship still exists, and in this case it is a little cool.

A third characteristic is that each relationship is different. You must build relationships with all kinds of people, regardless of race, religion, age, sex, or personality characteristics. Each relationship will be unique. Each will be built on a different basis. Each will have its own integrity.

As you look around and study your co-workers and your supervisor, it is easy to see that they are all different. They are all separate personalities. Even so, some individuals believe that *they* look the same to everyone around them. In other words, from the other side of the relationship, do you look the same to others?

Strange as it may seem, you do not.

You do not look the same to different people. Just as other people appear different to you, you appear different to other people. You make a different impression on each of them because they interpret you differently.

There is another way of saying this: you do not have a *single* personality in the eyes of others. Each person interprets you differently—based on his (or her) own unique background, prejudices, likes, dislikes, and so on. Your personality, to that person, is different. The way he interprets your personality *is* your personality to that person.

If you were to stand up for ten minutes in front of ten total strangers, and if each of them was then asked to write out in detail how he (or she) interpreted your personality, what kind of personality sketches would you receive? Would they be the same?

Would they be different? To be sure, they might all be favorable sketches, but they would not be the same. Each person would describe you as a slightly different person.

Why all this emphasis on the way in which people view your personality? How will this help you become more sensitive to human relationships?

Here is your answer. Because everybody sees you differently, you will have to build good relationships with different people differently. And make no mistake here. *Good relationships must be built.* They seldom come about automatically.

You will rarely build a strong, warm, or healthy relationship with two persons in the same way. You will always have to take into consideration the party at the other end of the relationship.

Some people are not going to interpret your personality favorably to start with. You are going to have to be sensitive enough to determine who these people are, and then you must build a good relationship with them on an individual basis. It is not easy to change a cool relationship to a warm one, yet you cannot afford to allow it to remain in an unhealthy state. You should make some effort to build it into a stronger relationship. To do this, you should consider the person at the other end of the relationship, and remember that he sees you differently than anyone else.

Now that you have a good picture of just what is meant by a "relationship," it is time to talk about the two kinds of relationships.

First we will discuss the *vertical working relationship.*

This is the relationship between you and your immediate supervisor. If you are already a supervisor it is the relationship between you and a subordinate. If, as a regular employee, you have two or more supervisors, you will have two or more vertical relationships to maintain. Normally, you will have one immediate supervisor, as illustrated below.

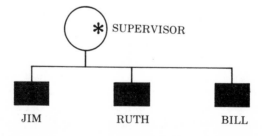

In a small department consisting of one supervisor and three employees, each employee has a different vertical relationship with the same supervisor. This relationship is indicated by the line between each employee and the supervisor. This is often called the *job-relations line*. If the relationship is strong, we indicate this by a heavy line. If it is weak, we indicate this by a light line. Naturally, it is almost impossible for the supervisor to create and maintain an equally strong line between himself and all employees in the department. It is his job to try to do this, and the closer he comes to this ideal the better it is for the department. But supervisors are human beings and are not perfect. Consequently, the job-relations lines are seldom equally strong. The person working next to you might have a stronger relationship with the supervisor than you have, or she might have a weaker one.

You will notice in the illustration below that arrows have been added to the lines.

These arrows at the ends of the vertical job-relations lines have real significance. They signify that there should be a free flow of information between the workers and the supervisor. It is extremely difficult for a strong relationship to exist between two persons without two-way communication. The supervisor must feel free to discuss, openly and frankly, certain problems with Ruth, Jim, and Bill. If the supervisor hesitates to talk with Jim about a certain weakness in his job performance, the relationship between the two of them is not what it could be. By the same token, if Jim is hesitant about taking a suggestion or a gripe to the supervisor, the relationship is less than ideal.

The lifeblood of a good relationship is free and open communication.
Good relationships are built and maintained by free and fre-

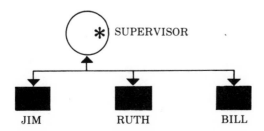

quent verbal communication. People need to talk with each other, exchange ideas, voice complaints, and offer suggestions if they intend to keep a good relationship. The moment that one party refuses to talk things over, the relationship line becomes thin and weak.

The primary responsibility for creating and maintaining a strong vertical relationship rests with the supervisor. This is a responsibility that goes with his position. If the relationship line is in need of repair, it is primarily his responsibility to initiate a discussion that can mend the break.

Although the supervisor has the primary responsibility, you as the employee have the secondary responsibility to keep the relationship line strong and healthy. Some employees make the serious mistake of thinking that the supervisor is wholly responsible for making them happy and productive.

A later chapter will show you how to create and maintain a good relationship with your supervisor. It will suffice now to say that you can't expect the supervisor to do all the relationship building. You will have to work hard to keep a good job-relations line between yourself and your supervisor. Even if you have an exceptionally poor supervisor, you will have to meet him (or her) halfway. Vertical relationships need to be in healthy repair if productivity is to be high in a department. Often the supervisor finds it a very delicate matter to keep it that way. Small wonder that management has seen fit to give him some special training.

The *horizontal working relationship* is also important to you. Horizontal working relationships are those that exist between you and fellow workers in the same department—the people you work next to on an hour-to-hour, day-to-day basis. The diagram below illustrates the horizontal relationships between three people in a very small department.

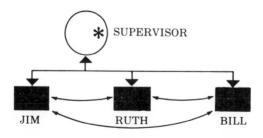

You will note that Jim has a horizontal working relationship with both Ruth and Bill. In this very small department of three employees and one supervisor, Jim has one vertical relationship and two horizontal relationships to keep strong. It is easy to see that in larger departments there would be many more. In fact, the larger the department you are assigned to, the more horizontal working relationships you must build and maintain.

You (not the supervisor) have the primary responsibility for creating and keeping healthy horizontal relationships. The supervisor—working at a long distance in regard to these relationships—has the secondary responsibility. Once in a while he might find it necessary to step in to help restore a good relationship between two employees. But by and large he must leave this up to the employees themselves. He is more an arbitrator when it comes to horizontal relationships.

The critical need for building good horizontal working relationships is often ignored by some workers. When they permit this to happen, their doors of opportunity are locked and the keys are thrown away.

It is extremely important to the new employee to build and maintain good horizontal working relationships. In fact, this should be a major part of your total human-relations effort as you start your career. Much of this book is devoted to the principles and techniques that will assist you in this respect. For example, here are two mistakes you should avoid.

1. Avoid concentrating on building a good relationship with your supervisor and neglecting good horizontal relationships with your fellow workers.

2. Avoid concentrating on building one or two very strong horizontal working relationships and neglecting those with the remaining fellow workers in your department.

Making either mistake will cause immediate disharmony in your department and will put you in human-relations hot water. The supervisor cannot afford to have an extremely strong relationship with you and weak relationships with your fellow workers if he wants high productivity from all. It makes for dissension and immediate cries of favoritism.

From your point of view, then, an overstrong vertical relationship can cause a general weakening of your horizontal working relationships. When you make the mistake of concentrating on one or two horizontal working relationships, the remaining horizontal relationships deteriorate and your vertical relationship with the supervisor is also weakened.

All horizontal working relationships in the same department should be given equal attention and consideration. One should not be strengthened at the expense of others, even though it may be more fun and more satisfying. Balance is important.

When you concentrate on creating good horizontal working relationships with all fellow workers, you almost always automatically create a good vertical relationship with your supervisor.

It should be recognized, of course, that the success of this principle is assured only if the supervisor is sufficiently sensitive to know what is going on. In the majority of cases this is a fair assumption. A perceptive supervisor will greatly appreciate any employee who builds a better team spirit in his department by creating and maintaining strong horizontal working relationships.

There are, of course, important relationships other than those indicated in the diagram. Your relationship-building activity should not be confined to a single department. For example, your supervisor has a boss and you should also build a good relationship with him or her. You should also develop relationships with other employees in other departments. You can even create good relationships with managers and supervisors in departments that are only indirectly connected with your own. You should pay special attention to creating friendly relationships with those people in the personnel department. You should also be careful not to neglect relationships with caretakers, custodians, guards, switchboard operators, secretaries, and many other people with whom you will have only limited contact. It is a good idea for you to expand your sphere of influence as quickly as possible on your new job. The more good relationships you build, the better.

If you are employed by a union organization you should not neglect or deliberately antagonize relationships because an individual is or is not a union member. If you are in management (nonunion) you should make an extra effort to build good working relationships with shop stewards, union agents, and union members. If you are a shop steward, union agent, or rank-and-file union member, you should, in turn, make a special effort to build good, two-way relationships with management people. The fact that management and labor may be in two different camps and need to negotiate problems makes the building of strong, open relationships more important, not less.

As important as these relationships are, however, they may not be your primary working relationships. You may have to build such relationships on an occasional or supplementary basis. Chance contacts, interdepartmental staff meetings, and telephone conversations are some of the opportunities you will have to do this. But remember: you cannot afford to concentrate on building relationships outside your department by neglecting those on the inside.

The building of a strong vertical relationship with your immediate supervisor and strong horizontal working relationships with your fellow workers is absolutely essential to your personal success. No other human-relations activity should have a higher priority.

PROBLEM 4
Decision

Bernie received his first assignment two days after joining the Elite Company. He was to be the junior member of the traffic department in which he would have seven horizontal relationships and one vertical relationship to build. All of the other employees, including the supervisor, were much older than he was.

After one week in the department, he discovered that his supervisor was difficult to approach or talk to, that he stayed aloof from the workers in the department, and that he often seemed critical. In fact, Bernie could feel a psychological barrier between the supervisor and the rest of the department. Once a week there was a short staff meeting, but most of the employees were silent and somewhat hostile.

How could he build a strong, worthwhile vertical relationship with a man of this nature in an environment that was so disciplined? After giving it some serious thought, he decided to concentrate almost exclusively on horizontal relationships. The supervisor seemed to be a lost cause, so why should he make any direct efforts to build a relationship the supervisor didn't seem to want anyway?

What result might such an effort have had? Was this a smart decision on Bernie's part? Would you have gone about it differently? Support your point of view. (For a suggested answer, see page 189.)

5

Productivity and Good Human Relations

Productivity, as we have seen, is a big word in the world of work. It is a word that management uses a great deal. It is a word that we need to understand better.

A manufacturing plant, in order to be competitive with other operations turning out a similar product, must *produce* at the lowest possible cost per single item or unit. A retail store, in order to pay overhead expenses and show a profit, must *produce* sales at a certain level. An airline must *produce* a reliable service that will attract enough customers to keep the seats filled. Even a governmental organization, like a fire department, must *produce* a level that will satisfy taxpayers. Every kind of organization must

"Some people aren't worth building relationships with!"

produce, and when production is not sufficient to make a profit or satisfy people, changes are made. These are economic and political facts.

Management, therefore, must be interested not only in the productivity of individuals, but also in that of divisions, departments, or branches. Management must be interested in order to survive. This is our free-enterprise system in operation.

Productivity is a difficult word to understand fully.

It means different things to different people, depending on the kind of organization one works for. Stated simply, it means on-the-job performance. The work you do. What you accomplish in an hour, a day, or a year.

Productivity for a salesperson in a department store means selling a certain amount of merchandise on a given day, doing a certain amount of stock work and clean-up activities, treating customers the right way, building good displays. Productivity not only means doing certain things; it also means *how* they are done.

Productivity to a telephone operator may mean handling a certain number of calls satisfactorily over a certain period.

Productivity to a needleworker in a garment factory may mean sewing on 780 sleeves in an eight-hour period. If the needleworker sews 780 sleeves, she is a good producer; if she sews 860, she is an outstanding producer; if she sews 640, she is a poor producer.

Productivity is a management word.

Management uses it to indicate the output or performance of people, departments, or machines. Because all organizations must be interested in profits, management is always interested in ways of increasing productivity. Because an increase in costs (wages, materials, transportation) can only be offset by an increase in price or productivity, the emphasis is to be expected.

Why has management gone out of its way during the past twenty years to improve employee cafeterias, lounge rooms, recreational facilities, lighting facilities, and countless other things?

There is but one answer: better employee morale that will result in greater productivity.

Because productivity is so important, management has devised ways of measuring it.

Productivity is easily measured on an assembly line where the worker must perform a specific function, such as connecting a wire or screwing on a nut. This kind of job can be time-studied and a certain standard rate can be established. If the standard rate is 85 completions in 60 minutes, it means that the average worker can reach and sustain this number over a certain period of time.

Measurable jobs or tasks of this nature are found primarily in the manufacturing and fabricating industries. Other jobs, such as that of a secretary, are more difficult to measure, because such factors as how much initiative is demonstrated, how people are treated, and how the telephone is answered, must be considered.

Productivity, then, can be measured scientifically in some situations, but in countless others it is measured by management judgment. Regardless of the kind of job you now hold or the way in which your productivity is measured, understanding what is meant by productivity (from the management point of view) is important to your future.

There are two kinds of productivity.

Individual productivity: This is a personal thing. It is the contribution a single person makes under certain working situations to getting the departmental job accomplished. It is the amount of work one person does in comparison to that of others in the group or section. It may or may not be measurable.

Group productivity: This is the sum total of all individual contributions, including that of the supervisor. It can be—and often is—measured objectively, that is, reduced to figures and statistics.

Each worker has a *current* (day-to-day, week-to-week) level of productivity that generally remains constant, although it may fluctuate from time to time. Let us illustrate this through the use of a glass or beaker. Let us assume that a solid line drawn across the glass is the *current* level of productivity for a person we will call Jane. Like all employees, Jane also has a *potential* level of productivity that is greater than her current level.

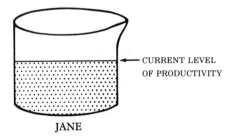

CURRENT LEVEL
OF PRODUCTIVITY

JANE

Seldom, if ever, does a person reach his or her full potential. Jane would be the first to agree with this. So let us draw a dotted line across the glass to indicate Jane's potential level of productivity. We don't know exactly where Jane's potential might be. It is impossible to measure her capacity or potential scientifically, because more than her mental ability is involved—and even her mental ability cannot be measured accurately. But for our hypothetical situation, we can say that Jane's potential is substantially above her current level of productivity.

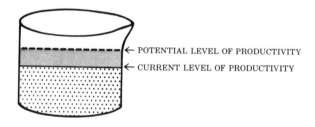

← POTENTIAL LEVEL OF PRODUCTIVITY
← CURRENT LEVEL OF PRODUCTIVITY

In the diagram below, then, Jane's current level of productivity is indicated by the solid line and her potential or possible level of productivity is indicated by the dotted line. The difference between the two is what we will call the *productivity gap*.

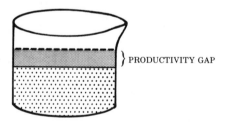

} PRODUCTIVITY GAP

There is always a gap between what one could do and what one actually does. Of course management would like to see Jane close the gap between her current and potential productivity levels as much as possible, but it would be asking too much to expect her to close it completely.

We are concerned, then, not so much with the gap itself as with the *size* of the gap. If it is small, Jane's supervisor knows she is working close to her capacity. If it is large, the supervisor knows that something is wrong and should be looked into.

Jane's supervisor should, of course, do all she can to keep the distance between Jane's potential and her current performance as small as possible. If the gap becomes too great, she might decide that Jane needs additional training, a special incentive, a change in assignment rotation, or perhaps some form of counseling. The supervisor cannot permit Jane's level of productivity to remain substandard over an extended period of time.

Jane, of course, is not the only worker in the department. In our imaginary situation, let us assume that there are two other employees occupying positions identical to Jane's. These people are called Art and Fred.

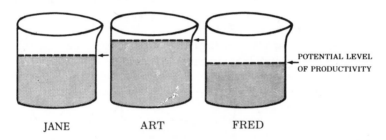

POTENTIAL LEVEL
OF PRODUCTIVITY

JANE   ART   FRED

You will note that the potentials of Art and Fred are different from Jane's. It is somewhat disturbing at first to recognize that everyone has his or her own potential and that some people have higher potentials than others. However, this is in fact true, because everyone has a different mental ability (IQ), ability to endure physical strain (stamina and endurance), ability to perform certain manipulative skills (aptitude), creative level, inner drive, and attitude, as well as other different personality characteristics. All of these features, added together, make up an individual's potential. As you can see, potential is much more than just mental ability.

It is important not to get hung up over the word *potential*. As we are using it, potential simply means the level of productivity a worker might achieve under ideal circumstances if he were pushing himself to his limit. It is seldom, if ever, reached. In using the word *potential*, however, we should remember that some employees are outstanding in some areas, and average or below in others. Few, if any, have characteristics that make them outstanding in all areas. Yet almost everyone has at least one exceptional characteristic.

We need not be technical about the word. We need only recognize that there are differences in capacity or potential between fellow workers. Some of it can be mental ability, but other characteristics also play an important role.

Nor need we be concerned about the measurement of such levels for our purposes, because there is no scientific way to do this. All that we need be concerned about is that individual differences exist and that, except under extremely rare conditions, there is always a gap between one's potential and what one is presently achieving.

In the diagram below, Art has been arbitrarily given a potential above Jane's and Fred's. Fred, on the other hand, has been given a potential below Jane's and Art's.

Now, to complete our diagram, let us assign a current productivity level to each of the three workers.

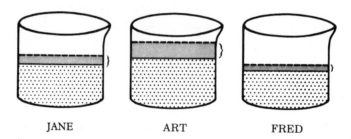

JANE   ART   FRED

You will note that, even though Art has a higher potential than Jane, there is not a substantial difference between their current levels of performance. This is a compliment to Jane and perhaps indicates that she is more highly motivated to succeed and consequently performs closer to her potential.

Fred also deserves a compliment, because the gap between his current level of productivity and his potential is smaller than that for either Jane or Art. Fred is doing an excellent job in living up to his potential. Perhaps with more education and training, Fred will be able to raise his potential gradually and, in turn, increase his productivity. In our hypothetical situation, however, Fred could not be expected to increase his productivity substantially.

If you study this simple diagram, you will discover many pro-
vocative points of discussion. Just imagine the many variations
and complications that would arise if the diagram were to include
twelve employees instead of three. Even the premise that a person
can raise his or her potential through education and training is
debatable. Our concern, however, is the relation between a person's occupational potential and actual level of performance.

Just as each individual has a current and potential level of productivity, so does each branch, division, or department of an
organization. This we call *group productivity.*

The diagram below illustrates this important concept. The
glass or beaker represents the productivity level and potential of
the department as a whole. Let us combine the productivity levels
of Jane, Art, and Fred and that of their supervisor in a departmental diagram.

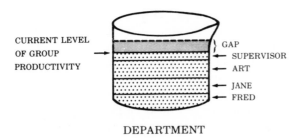

DEPARTMENT

You will observe that the productivity levels of Fred, Jane, and
Art (from the previous chart) have been added to that of the supervisor. As you can see, the supervisor does not contribute as
much in productivity (actually getting the work out) as do the
individual employees. How can this be?

The answer is simple. The primary responsibility of the supervisor is to help each worker achieve *his or her* maximum productivity. The supervisor's secondary responsibility (as a working
supervisor) is to get a certain amount of work done himself. He
(or she) cannot be expected to take care of his many supervisory
responsibilities and also do as much work as one of the employees
in his department. His concern is the *total departmental productivity,* for this is how he is measured by management.

You will also notice that there is a gap in this chart just as there
was in the others. This is a *departmental gap.* Just as an individual

has a certain potential for productivity, so does a department. A crew working for a telephone company might have the potential for installing 120 telephones per day, and yet they might install only 80. A department inside a retail store might have the potential for selling $5,000 worth of merchandise on a given day when everything is ideal, and yet on most days they might sell only $2,000 worth. A claims department for an insurance company might have the potential for processing 50 claims per day, and yet they may never reach this goal. Just as there is a gap with individuals, there is also one with departments.

It is the responsibility of the individual to try and close the gap between what he or she is currently producing and what he or she can ideally produce. It is the responsibility of the supervisor to close the gap btween what his department is currently doing and what it might do in the future.

There are two ways in which a supervisor can do this. One is by working harder himself, putting in more hours and making better use of his time. Since he is only one person, there is a limit to what he could do by himself to reduce the size of the gap.

The second—and by far the more effective way to reduce the gap—is to reduce the gaps between the levels of each employee. The productivity of the department is the sum total of the productivity of all members of the department, including the supervisor. The supervisor is interested in each worker's productivity because of what each can contribute to the total.

What should this basic principle mean to you?

Simply this: all employees in a department are interdependent as far as departmental productivity is concerned. If you raise your personal productivity, but at the same time take away some of the productivity of others in the department (because of poor human relations), you have not necessarily added to the total.

Sound strange?

To demonstrate this vital fundamental, let us take Art as an example. The diagram at the top of the next page tells us that Art has a high potential and a good level of productivity. In fact, he is currently producing more than both Jane and Fred.

But let us assume for a moment that Art begins to ignore Jane and Fred. He is no longer interested in helping them. He refuses to pitch in and do some of their work when they are absent. He starts to rub them the wrong way. His superior attitude causes

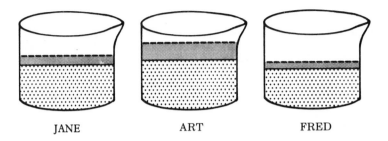

JANE   ART   FRED

resentment. Instead of natural, healthy competition the situation becomes personal and vindictive.

What could happen then?

The productivity of Jane and Fred could drop due to departmental disharmony. The diagram below illustrates what might happen.

The gap between what Jane and Fred can each do and what they are now doing has widened. Even though Art has maintained his *personal* level of productivity, *the departmental productivity level has dropped.*

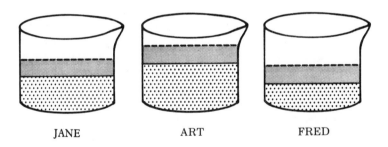

JANE   ART   FRED

Now let us see what might happen if Art does just the opposite. Let us assume that he becomes more sensitive about human relations. Instead of antagonizing Jane and Fred, he starts working *with* them. He helps them on their off days. He takes up some of the slack when they are absent. He compliments them on certain skills. He earns their respect instead of their animosity. What happens? Harmony replaces disharmony.

Instead of a wider gap between the current and potential productivity levels of Jane and Fred, there is a smaller gap. Both Jane and Fred produce more because Art has strengthened his

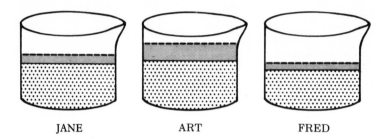

JANE   ART   FRED

horizontal relationships with them. As you can see above, *the departmental productivity level has increased.*

This interdependence between workers in a department cannot be ignored. *Group* productivity is the key more than *individual* productivity.

It should be pointed out, however, that sometimes a single individual can raise his or her productivity above that of co-workers and, even though relationships are not ideal, the co-workers will strive to increase their personal productivity so that the other worker will not show them up. The reaction of employees in each situation is different.

Let's review what we have discussed in this chapter.

You have learned that there is always a gap between an individual's current level of productivity and his or her potential. If the employee consistently has a small gap, he is trying hard to contribute and should be complimented by his supervisor for working close to his potential.

You have learned that there is a departmental gap that represents the difference between what a department can do and what it actually is doing. If the departmental gap is small, the supervisor is doing a good job and should be complimented by his superiors.

You have also learned that because of the way people react to each other (human relations), one worker can influence the productivity of others and therefore either lower or increase the productivity of the entire department. In other words, it is possible for an employee to increase his (or her) *personal* productivity but decrease *departmental* productivity because of his poor human-relations skills.

This may sound illogical or contradictory, but give it some serious thought. Most experts agree that there is a definite relationship between human-relations competence and productivity.

PROBLEM 5
Message

Jeff was one of several employees in a small department where productivity depended upon the close cooperation of everyone involved. He had a high potential and lived up to it. Because of this, he personally produced more than anyone else in the department.

But Jeff happened to be the kind of individual who liked to work alone. He seldom volunteered to help his fellow workers. Many of the people who had to work with him felt he had a superior attitude, and they resented it. As a result, the department was split between Jeff and the others. There was little team spirit.

Jeff's supervisor gave a lot of thought to the problem and looked at it this way. Although Jeff was producing at the highest level in the department, the total productivity of the department had not gone up since he joined the group. Instead it had gone down slightly. Could it be that Jeff had done more damage (through his poor human relations) than he had done good (by his high personal productivity)? The supervisor came to the conclusion that Jeff was an outstanding employee when viewed alone. But he was a very poor employee when viewed as a member of a group.

A few weeks later, the supervisor was promoted to a more responsible position and management had to come up with a replacement. They decided to promote someone from outside the department. When Jeff discovered that he was not chosen, he demanded an explanation. He was told that he was the highest producer in the department but his human-relations skills were not up to standard. Management felt the other workers in the department would not respect him as their supervisor.

Do you agree with management's decision to pass over Jeff even though Jeff was the best producer? Give reasons why you agree or disagree. How responsible do you feel the supervisor was for Jeff's being passed over? (For a suggested answer, see page 189.)

Factors
Management Seeks

There is a danger of misinterpretation in discussing human relations and productivity. You might have deduced from the last few chapters that building strong and healthy vertical and horizontal working relationships automatically results in greater departmental productivity. This is not necessarily so.

An employee can be happy, satisfied, and content with his (or her) job and yet not carry his fair share of the work load. A group of employees in a department can be getting along beautifully with each other, and yet the productivity of the department might be far below average.

Happy employees are usually—but not always—high producers.

Therefore, the goal of good human relations is not just happy employees, but *happy employees that produce more.* The goal is greater productivity and ultimately a greater net profit. It is theoretically possible that a business organization could devote so

"High productivity and good relationships too?"

much time and money to making employees happy and comfortable that the company could go broke and out of business. Management is therefore not interested in making people happy just because happy people are nice to have around or stick with their jobs longer. Management is interested in making its employees happy because happy employees, under the right leadership, can be motivated to greater productivity.

This should not be interpreted as meaning that employers are sensitive to their employees' needs *only* in terms of greater productivity. This is not true. Nevertheless, management (and their employees) must fully accept the economic truth that survival under free competition requires a continual improvement in personal and group productivity. If product prices are to remain stable, increases in wages, greater fringe benefits, better working conditions, and improved physical facilities are possible only when there is an increase in productivity to accompany them.

The employee who is fun to be around but never gets down to doing his share of the work is a burden on his fellow workers. He is a parasite on the productivity of others. He may be pleasant to have around, but he is far too expensive for management to keep.

The work itself must be done.

Labor costs must be controlled.

Customers must be well served.

Greater productivity must be the goal of American business organizations if they are to survive and compete with other world markets where labor costs are much lower. The development and use of more and more highly technical equipment will take us a long way, but human productivity must do the rest.

It is only natural, then, that management should seek outstanding people for jobs that are increasingly sophisticated. It is only natural that they should try to find, hire, and train people who have already developed their human-relations skills to a high level.

What are the human factors management seeks?

The most important one is the *right combination of personal productivity and human relations*. The best way to explain this fundamental is to present another hypothetical situation.

This time we will assume that there is a small department composed of three employees who have identical assignments and similar work loads. We will further assume that Alice and Richard have been employed in their positions for over a year. Hazel, on the other hand, joined the organization yesterday as a replacement for an employee who had resigned. She has a very high potential, substantially above that of either of the other two people.

Alice and Richard have been taking it very easy in the department, and there has been a sizable gap between their current level of productivity and their potentials. In other words, they have not been motivated to do the kind of job they can do. Hazel, however, is very ambitious. She wants to build a reputation for herself and, if possible, move on quickly to a supervisory position where she will have more responsibility and remuneration. She wants to experience a long-term personal growth pattern within the organizational structure. In order to start her climb into management, Hazel has decided that it will be necessary for her to increase her personal level of productivity to the point where it will be above that of Alice and Richard. She has decided she can do this in either of two ways:

1. She could go about it very quickly. She could go all out and pass Alice and Richard in a hurry. But in using this approach she would risk building poor horizontal working relationships with her fellow workers.

2. She could pass Alice and Richard in personal productivity on a somewhat slower and less obvious schedule. This way she could concentrate on building good horizontal relationships with her fellow workers and create a harmonious environment that would increase *their* productivity along with her own.

What might happen if Hazel decided to follow the first approach and ignore building good horizontal relationships?

It is possible, of course, that Alice and Richard might become motivated. Perhaps in order to make their positions more secure they might compete with Hazel, and as a result the productivity of the entire department might increase.

It is also possible that many unfortunate things could happen. Alice and Richard might resent Hazel, and rather than work with her they could, in subtle ways, work against her. For example, because they are more experienced, they might let her make some mistakes that they could prevent if they wanted to. They could do many little things that would make her uncomfortable and her work more difficult. As a result, Hazel might become critical of Alice and Richard, and the relationships between the three could deteriorate to a point where the productivity of all three would drop. This would be especially obvious if customers were involved.

This might not happen, of course—but it could happen! And if it did, Hazel would certainly not have helped her future with the company. It is not a safe approach for her to take. She could be asking for trouble.

Now what might happen if Hazel took the opposite approach —if she passed Alice and Richard in personal productivity but at the same time worked hard to build good, strong working relationships with them?

It is likely that Hazel would make her job easier. She would be valued more by the supervisor. She would earn the support of both Alice and Richard. She would contribute more to productivity. Instead of falling into a human-relations trap, she would demonstrate to management that she had insight and sensitivity.

Of course, it would be easy to tell Hazel that building good working relationships with Alice and Richard is the best route to take. But how should she go about doing it? Here are four suggestions.

1. Hazel could build better horizontal relationships with Alice and Richard if she would sacrifice a little of her personal productivity to help increase theirs. She could accomplish this by looking for opportunities to help Alice and Richard when their work load is heavy or when they do not feel well. She could also pitch in when one is absent.

2. As Hazel brings her personal productivity above that of Alice and Richard, she should be careful not to become critical of them because their performance levels are now lower than hers. She should not expect continual praise from her supervisor just because she is, at this point in her career, carrying a larger share of the work load.

3. Hazel should be careful not to isolate herself too much from Alice and Richard. Even if she is occasionally rejected by them, she must continue to be pleasant until good relationships are

built. She must be sincerely interested in both Alice and Richard as individuals in order to win their respect. A superior attitude on her part will defeat any effort she makes to build sound relationships.

4. Above all, Hazel should stand on her own two feet and work out her own problems without complaining or running to the supervisor for help. She can only achieve the support of Alice and Richard by demonstrating to them that she knows what she is doing and can fight her own battles.

Hazel will go a long way in communicating to management that she has one of the *human-relations plus factors* they seek if she keeps the following principle in mind. *An increase in personal productivity should be accompanied by increased attention to horizontal relationships.*

You might feel that all of this is expecting too much of Hazel or of any new employee who is ambitious and wishes to improve her position with an organization. Perhaps. But doesn't it really depend on how important personal progress is to the individual? If Hazel were to jog along with Alice and Richard, she might not be sufficiently motivated to give such a plus factor to her job. But since she wishes to qualify for better opportunities, it is a price she should be willing to pay. Personal productivity is only one of many plus factors, and it is not enough to take Hazel as far as she wishes to go. She must also be human-relations competent.

Last week Hazel was invited to have a long talk with the personnel director of her company. During the conversation she asked the personnel director what kind of a person management was really seeking. The personnel director said that management usually sought four plus factors in the employees they hoped to promote into management. Hazel made a big effort to remember all four, and this is the way she would probably put it if you asked her now.

• *The person management is looking for is someone who strives to work close to her (or his) personal potential regardless of the level at which her fellow workers are performing.* She is always trying to close her personal productivity gap even though others are content to do only what they have to in order to keep their jobs. She is self-motivating. She is not satisfied to drag along. She abhors mediocrity in a person who has a high potential. She takes a professional approach to her job and gains real satisfaction when she does it well.

• *She is never completely satisfied with her personal potential.* She believes that she can always improve it a little. She truly believes in lifelong learning. She takes advantage of any training that the company will provide. She continues to read and study on her own. She is always learning more and more about the job ahead of her. She may even continue her formal education by attending classes at a nearby adult education center, junior or senior college, or university. Although she is realistic about her potential, she does not agree with those who say it cannot be improved. She does not go along with the idea that a person is born with a certain potential that cannot be changed. She will continue to learn and to prepare for new opportunities.

To put it another way, the person management is looking for refuses to put her potential on the shelf. She wants to raise it higher and higher, so that she will be ready for future opportunities. She does not resent others who have higher potentials. She simply wants to make the most of her own potential.

• *She believes human relations is very important.* She puts people and the development of good human-relations skills ahead of machines, statistics, procedures, and credentials. She accepts the responsibility of building strong relationships as an interesting and inevitable challenge. She is highly productive, and at the same time she protects her relationships with people. She does this with a sense of humor and personal understanding. She is proud of the fact that she is a good person to work next to. She doesn't overplay her hand by becoming mushy or flowery in her approach to others. She endeavors to keep all relations on a sincere level. She does all of this because she knows that she contributes to the productivity of her department in two ways: one, through her own personal work effort; and two, through the relationships she builds with her fellow employees. She refuses to sacrifice one for the other, and she constantly tries to keep them in proper balance.

• *She makes a point of being loyal to her company or organization.* This does not mean that she automatically accepts all of the policies and practices that filter down from the top. Far from it. She accepts the responsibility of making changes, but she remains loyal to her company while fighting to bring such changes about. She feels that her company deserves her best effort. She refuses to let human-relations problems, the negative attitudes of others, or personal disappointments slow her down. She sets goals for herself, but if she does not reach those goals according to her own time schedule, she does not become overly disturbed. She knows that she will probably accomplish her life's work inside an organizational framework, so she studies things carefully and tries to be patient and see the whole picture.

Hazel asked the personnel director a second question: "How many employees will I find in this company that have all of the four plus factors?"

He replied: "It is impossible to say. There are many who are good at one or two, some who are good at three, but only a very few who are good at all four. At any rate, those who demonstrate all four do not remain line employees for long, unless by choice, because they are desperately needed for supervisory positions."

Hazel then followed with her last question: "How does management single out those who have the plus factors they seek?"

"It's very easy," replied the director. "You only have to be slightly taller than others to stand out in a crowd. It's the same with the plus factors. You don't have to be miles ahead of others for management to recognize you; a little is all it takes."

PROBLEM 6
Insight

Ted had been with the Kramer Corporation for more than nine months. From his first day, he had been determined to set a pace that would earn him a promotion. It took him a little while to catch on to the job, but within four months he was up to the average of others in productivity. After a few more months he was the top producer in the department. In the meantime, the others maintained a steady, but slower, pace.

Ted felt good about his ability to pass others in the department, but he was disturbed because he had received so little recognition for the achievement. In fact, the harder he worked, the more difficult it was to get along with the others. Even the supervisor had failed to give Ted as much encouragement as he felt he deserved.

After a few weeks of being the top producer, Ted started to become more critical of the others. He started to give out a few tips on how they might improve their efficiency, and he began to sound off more in staff meetings.

One day the whole situation reached a boiling point. Ted was strongly counseled by his supervisor to be more patient and understanding with his fellow workers. "Look, Ted," said his supervisor. "You've got it all going for you, but you will never win a promotion if you blow your cool with your fellow employees. You have a very high potential and your productivity is great, but you can't expect others to always equal your pace. I don't want you to destroy now the very relationships you might have to rebuild later should you take my place."

Was Ted's exasperation justified? Or did his supervisor have a good point? (For a suggested answer, see page 190.)

7

Your Most Important Working Relationship

The most important working relationship you must deal with is the one between you and your immediate supervisor. This single relationship can speed up your personal progress or slow it down to a discouraging crawl. It can make going to work a joy or a drag. It can prepare you for greater responsibilities or it can frustrate your desire to learn. And there is just no way to avoid the human-relations fact that your supervisor is a VIP—a Very Important Person—whom, good or bad, you must learn to cope with.

What kind of a person will you draw as a supervisor?

It is impossible to predict. However, he (or she) will be basically the same person he used to be when he held a job similar to yours, except that now he has much more responsibility. He

"Yes, sir, I understand my supervisor perfectly."

may or may not have been given some special training to help him become a good supervisor. He may be easy to get along with, or he may be very difficult. He may be sensitive to your needs, or he may be insensitive. He may be feeling his way along and making many mistakes, or he may be highly experienced and a real pro at his job.

Three things are certain about your supervisor, however: (1) he probably has a strong personality that gave him the confidence to become a supervisor in the first place; (2) the responsibilities of being a supervisor probably weigh heavily on his shoulders, and (3) he has work authority over you.

What is a supervisor?

He is a *teacher*. He will not only teach you the routine of your new job, but he will also have a great influence on your attitude toward your job and the company. He has a reservoir of knowledge, skills, and techniques that you need to learn. You will be most fortunate if he is a good teacher. If he is not, you will have to learn from observation.

He is a *counselor*. His job is to see that you live up to your potential. He may need to correct errors you are making. He may need to give you tips on improving yourself as an employee. He may feel the need to have a heart-to-heart talk with you at times.

He is a *leader*. More than anything else, your supervisor must provide the leadership your department requires. He must see that you are happy and productive, but he cannot neglect others in the department. He must provide motivation for all employees. He must earn your respect—not by being soft and easy, but by being a strong leader who will help you build a long-range career.

It would be a mistake to attempt to type supervisors. They cannot be clearly classified into different groups. Each supervisor has a unique personality. He will operate under his own system just as your teachers did.

Do you recall your early school days when you discovered the differences between teachers? You may have had one who expected a great deal more from you than the others did. At the time you may not have liked this person, yet, years later, he or she may have become your favorite. The same can be true with supervisors.

When you start a new job you don't want an easygoing supervisor who does not care and, as a result, will hurt instead of help your future. You will be better off with a more concerned, more demanding supervisor who will help you reach your potential. With an easy supervisor you might develop some poor working habits and eventually become unhappy with yourself. With a stronger supervisor, one who will take time to train you, you will become a better worker and improve your future. But no matter what kind of a boss you encounter, it is up to you to learn to understand him and work efficiently under his kind of leadership.

You should do some of the adjusting.

You should provide some of the understanding.

You should help in building the relationship that must exist between the two of you.

Each individual supervisor creates his own special climate, or atmosphere, under which you must operate. The following analysis of three kinds of climates may give you some indication of the adjustments you might have to make in the future.

The Structured Climate

Some supervisors are more strict than others. They operate a very tight department by keeping very close, and sometimes restrictive, controls. They frequently expect employees to be precisely on time, orderly, and highly efficient. They permit foolishness only when a very special occasion calls for it. Ninety-eight percent of the time they stick strictly to business.

The supervisor who creates this kind of atmosphere often appears cold, distant, and unfeeling to the new employee. He (or she) seems unreachable. He seems unreasonable. As a result, the new employee may begin to fear him.

Some jobs force supervisors to be autocratic. Some kinds of work require a very high level of safety standards and efficiency. For example, a supervisor of telephone operators might have to be autocratic in order to maintain the level of split-second efficiency that this job requires. Work of a highly technical nature in which certain precision standards must be met will call for a different climate than work that is primarily in a service field.

Although the supervisor who establishes this kind of atmosphere may appear cold and unapproachable, the direct opposite may be true. He is probably more interested in you and more willing to help you than you suspect. One must not be afraid of a supervisor of this kind. It may take more time to build a meaningful relationship with him, but once achieved, that relationship may be more valuable. Adjusting to a structured or autocratic climate is not easy for many young workers, especially those who have not been exposed to it before.

The Permissive Climate

The direct opposite of the structured climate is the permissive atmosphere. Some supervisors are very free and easy in creating a working climate. They provide little or no direct leadership. There is an absence of intervention. It is a loose situation with few controls or restrictions.

This permissive climate can be the most dangerous of all for the new employee, because his (or her) need for self-discipline is so great. If he does not feel the presence of a leader, he may not make good use of his time. If he is given very little encouragement, he may find it difficult to motivate himself. If things are so easygoing, he may relax too much and become too friendly with fellow workers. All of this can cause bad habits that can lead to mutual dissatisfaction. Instead of being an ideal situation, then, the permissive climate becomes a trap that can destroy the desire to succeed and eventually cause great unhappiness.

Whether we like to accept it or not, strong but sensitive leadership gives us more job security and forces us to live closer to our potential. In most cases, a little too much may be better than very little. Beware of a climate that is too relaxed unless you are a self-starter and can discipline yourself. You might discover that too much freedom is your downfall.

The Democratic Climate

The goal of most supervisors in modern organizations is to create a democratic climate. This atmosphere is the most difficult of all to establish. In fact, purely democratic action is often a goal rather than a reality.

A democratic climate is one in which the employees *want* to do what the supervisor wants done. The supervisor becomes one of the group and still retains his (or her) leadership role. He permits the employees to have a great deal to say about the operation of the department. Everyone becomes involved, because each person works from inside the group rather than from outside. The supervisor is the leader and a member of the group at the same time. As a result, a team feeling is created. Many isolated cases of research indicate that most people will respond with greater personal satisfaction and greater productivity if the supervisor can create and maintain a democratic atmosphere.

If this is true, why can't more supervisors achieve this kind of climate? There are many reasons.

In the first place, it is the most difficult to create, and once it is created it is far more difficult to maintain. It requires a real expert, an individual with great skill and sensitivity; one should not expect to find a great number of supervisors with this ability.

In the second place, not all workers will respond to this climate, ideal as it may seem. *You* may like it best, but others in your department may like a more autocratic approach. This is especially true when there are younger workers in a department where many more experienced and older employees work. You will often hear employees say: "I wish he would quit fooling around and *tell* us what to do" or "I wish she would tighten up things around here—those people are getting away with murder" or "He is too easy. I can't enjoy working for someone who doesn't set things down clearly and specifically from the beginning."

In the third place, the supervisor who aspires to build a true democratic climate always finds himself (or herself) somewhere between the structured and the permissive. He may approach the ideal situation for a while, only to find that a few employees are taking advantage of him. When this happens it is necessary to tighten up again and become more structured.

All supervisors must create and maintain what some people refer to as a *discipline line*. This is an imaginary line or point beyond which the employee senses she or he should not pass lest some form of disapproval and possible disciplinary action take place. Most management people claim that it is best for a new supervisor to start out with a firm discipline line and perhaps relax it a little later. They point out that if a discipline line becomes too low and undefined, things can get out of control. It is important to keep a consistent discipline line. Some supervisors claim that keeping a firm but comfortable one is a tightrope they walk each day on the job.

In recent years, management has been paying a great deal of attention to what it calls Theory X and Theory Y.

Theory X represents management by control. It states that the worker must be directed, motivated, and controlled in order to achieve high productivity. A basic assumption is that most employees are not self-motivated. The Theory X leadership style creates a more structured working climate. The discipline line is somewhat higher and tighter.

Theory Y represents participative management. It states that the worker will achieve greater productivity if he (or she) can set his own goals and direct his own efforts through involvement. This theory assumes that under the proper working climate workers will motivate themselves. The Theory Y leadership style creates a more permissive and democratic climate. The discipline line is lower but still well-defined.

Every supervisor creates his or her own individual climate. Some supervisors come up with a workable blend of the structured and democratic. Others come up with a blend of the permissive and democratic. Still others have a special blend that is all their own. We call this their *leadership style.*

Whether we personally like a supervisor or his style is not as important as whether we can learn to be productive in the climate he creates. The new worker should not be too quick to judge, however, because it is often true that what appears to be a difficult climate at the beginning might turn out to be a comfortable and beneficial one later on.

For example, one of the best things your supervisor can do is to go to bat for you with upper management. The communication that takes place between your supervisor and management concerning you and your progress is often the key to your future success. It is quite possible that a supervisor will expect a great deal from you, criticize you, even make you unhappy at times. But when the chips are down, this person could be the first to go to bat for you.

It is always good to remember that your supervisor also has a boss and that he must sometimes be more demanding than he wishes because of orders from above. Your supervisor may be under more pressure than you suspect, and although he may try to absorb it to protect you, he may not always be successful.

So what kind of a supervisor might you run into on your first assignment?

It is to be hoped, of course, that you draw a sensitive supervisor who can create a comfortable climate, provide the right amount of leadership to meet your needs, and help you reach your full potential. Chances are fairly good this will happen, but don't bank on it. Something quite different could possibly occur.

Pam, for example, started her career working for a supervisor who made a play for her. She had to fight him off for days until he finally reversed himself and started treating her the way he should have at the beginning. It was a difficult period for Pam, and only because she stood her ground forcefully and openly was she able to live through it and keep her positive attitude.

Roberto discovered rather quickly that his boss was frequently drunk on the job, and management either did not know about it or chose to overlook it. As a result, Roberto and his fellow workers often had to take a great deal of abuse. Some days the supervisor even disappeared for long periods, and they had to get the work out without his help. All of this caused Roberto to take a very critical view of all supervisors, but fortunately this supervisor was eventually transferred to another department and his replacement was so good that Roberto's faith was soon restored.

Perhaps Ryan's first supervisor was even more difficult to deal with than the two described above. This one played one employee against the other so that nobody in the department knew where he or she stood. He would have a favorite for a few days and then, without provocation, reject this person and switch to another. Finally it became obvious to management that productivity was in a nosedive and would not improve, so they took action. The new supervisor was everything Ryan could have wanted, but it took him a long time to forget his first unfortunate experience.

The above examples, to be sure, are not typical. Most supervisors are sensitive, sincere, and serious people who will do their best to build a strong, healthy relationship with you. But whether you draw a good, bad, or indifferent supervisor, it will be your responsibility to build the best possible relationship with him or her. To help you meet this challenge, here are ten tips that should help you.

1. *Avoid transferring to your supervisor negative attitudes you may have developed toward other authority figures in your life.* Some young people who have had problems with parents, older brothers and sisters, teachers, police, and similar authority figures make the mistake of transferring their feelings of hostility to their first supervisor, simply because she (or he) represents another authority figure. This is unfair to the supervisor and is the worst possible way to get started on a new job. Wipe away any previous negative feelings you may have and give your new boss a free, honest opportunity to build a healthy relationship with you. Her role is much different from that of other authority figures because she is primarily interested only in your on-the-job performance. If you give her a fair chance, she will almost always earn your respect instead of your hostility.

2. *Whenever possible, take the positive approach and try to make your supervisor look good.* Except under rare circumstances where the behavior of your supervisor does not deserve it, you will be smart to make your supervisor look good, because your success, to some extent, depends upon hers (or his). Indirectly, when you put her in a good light you automatically help yourself. For example, if your boss receives a promotion, two things might happen to you: (1) if you are the best available candidate, you might be promoted to her job; or (2) she might go to bat for you from her new, more strategic position. Normally speaking, if you have the right relationship with your supervisor, the more successful she becomes the more chance you too will have to advance.

3. *Expect some rough days under her supervision.* Everyone, including supervisors, is entitled to a few bad days. Your boss is only human. If she should boil over on a given day, don't let it throw you. If she seems to be picking on you for a while, give her time to get over it. More important than anything else, try not to take personally anything she does that you don't like. There may be times when you do not understand your boss's behavior, but if you can float along with it, chances are good that it won't last long.

4. *Refuse to nurse a small gripe into a major issue.* A small gripe, when nurtured, can get blown out of proportion and can lead to a confrontation with your supervisor that will hurt your relationship. If you have a legitimate gripe, try to talk it over with her

quickly so that you can get it out of your system before it builds up. It will take some initiative on your part to do this, and you must be sensitive enough to select the right time. But it is the best posture to take. Remember: she won't know you have a complaint unless you tell her.

5. *Select the right time to approach your supervisor.* Whether you have a complaint or a positive suggestion to make, try to approach your supervisor at the right time. She may be too busy or under too much pressure on a given day to talk to you. If so, wait it out. When the pressure is off, chances are good that she will give you a fair opportunity. However, if you do try to talk to her at a bad time—and are turned off—wait until another day and try again. If it is important to you, she will no doubt want to talk to you about it. Give her another chance.

6. *Never go above your supervisor's head without talking to her first.* The easiest and quickest way to destroy your relationship with your supervisor is to go over her head on a problem that involves her or her department. Always talk to your supervisor first. If you are not satisfied with the results, you can then take other action. At least this way your supervisor will know that you consulted her first.

7. *Try not to let your supervisor intimidate you.* Fear is a strong emotion. If you are so fearful of your boss that you cannot approach her, you should talk to personnel, consider a possible transfer, or if necessary resign. You will never be happy working for a person you fear, and a supervisor will seldom respect you if you are afraid of her.

8. *It can be a human-relations mistake to make a buddy of your supervisor.* Your relationship with your supervisor is a business relationship. Keep it that way. The distance between you and your boss may often appear to be a fine line, but she is still your boss. If you get too personal, it will almost always turn out badly.

9. *It will help if you apologize to your supervisor when you make a mistake.* Everyone makes mistakes. If you make a serious goof and injure your relationship with your boss, why not clean the slate with an honest apology? It is a good idea to leave work every day with a pleasant feeling toward your job and your supervisor. If you have had trouble with her on a given day and truly believe

that it is partially your fault, the mature thing to do is to accept your share of the blame. You will feel better and so will your supervisor.

10. *Remember that not all supervisors enjoy their roles.* A surprising number of supervisors would really prefer to be workers, but they have accepted their promotions because they feel they can contribute more as supervisors or because they can make more money. As an employee, you should view this as a possibility. It will give you more insight into the role itself and perhaps help you tolerate your supervisor more. Try to remember that being a good supervisor is difficult. Sometimes those who try the hardest to win the respect of their workers never fully succeed because of personality traits they cannot change.

In summary, building and maintaining a strong, warm, productive relationship with your boss is a real human-relations challenge. It isn't always easy. Yet it is an essential step in your progress. You may get used to one supervisor only to discover that you have been transferred to another department and have to start from scratch. Every relationship will be a unique challenge. Make the most of every experience.

PROBLEM 7
Choice

Carol is a career employee with a large organization. For the last sixty days she has been training for a new position and assignment. She has just received word to report to the personnel department to discuss her new role in the company.

The personnel director gives her a choice of assignments. She tells Carol that two departments have requested her services. The departments are identical in their operations. The only difference is between the supervisors of the two departments and the type of climate each creates. Carol is given the opportunity to observe both supervisors in action.

One department has a rather demanding supervisor who leans in the direction of Theory X. He believes in rather rigid performance standards and controls. He is an old-timer and has been in charge of his department for many years. He expects and gets high productivity and loyalty from all his employees. Everyone admits that he has trained more people who are now in top management positions than anyone in the company.

The other department is run by a younger supervisor who adheres to Theory Y. She tries to get everyone in the department to participate in decisions and get involved. She prides herself on her democratic approach and feels she has been very successful. People appear very happy working for her. The personnel turnover is less in this department than in the other. Productivity is almost, but not quite, as high.

Which department would you select? On what basis? (For a suggested answer, see page 191.)

Relationship
Characteristics

The purpose of this chapter is to look more deeply into the nature of working relationships. To do this we will explore seven different characteristics that are often involved. These characteristics can have a considerable influence on the quality or tone of the relationship. In a sense, they constitute the ingredients or components that make up the relationship itself.

Perhaps you will understand the idea of a relationship better if you visualize it as an invisible tunnel between two fellow employees. Disregard the personalities involved and concentrate on the relationship itself. The illustrations on the following page may help you do this.

The two-way arrows between the amoebas remind us that verbal communication is the lifeblood of the relationship. Good in-

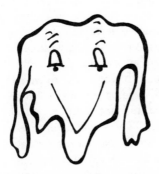

"You can't build perfect relationships with everybody."

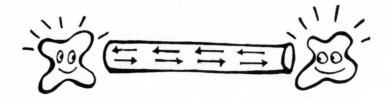

put and good reception are necessary at both ends. The illustration below adds to the relationship those factors we will deal with in this chapter.

Of course, not all of the above elements are likely to be present in any single relationship. Some relationships may have only one or two. Others may have four or five. An investigation into each of the above, however, will give you additional insight into the nature of all working relationships.

Value conflicts: Everyone has his or her own value system. Everyone has his own priority list as far as what is really important in life. Different people seek different life-styles. Because of this, it is only natural that value conflicts exist between people who have been forced to associate with each other closely in the world of work. Here are two typical examples.

Tony was assigned to work next to Mr. Henderson, who was more than twice his age. Tony was a bachelor who enjoyed an active social life and did not want to assume family responsibilities too soon in life. Tony was determined to come up with a life-style different from that of his parents. His fancy foreign sports car and fashionable clothing reflected this attitude. Mr. Henderson, on the other hand, was a family-oriented, religious person.

How did they learn to work together gracefully? At the beginning they both played it cool and built their relationship exclusively on job factors. Tony learned to respect Mr. Henderson for his many years of job experience and his willingness to share it. Mr. Henderson learned to respect Tony for his willingness to learn and contribute a full day's work. After six months they could even discuss their value differences. A better mutual understanding was brought about.

Beverley was brought up in a strict home environment and was taught to respect discipline. She was considered fairly square by her contemporaries. Trish, on the other hand, was very happy-go-lucky and undisciplined. She considered herself very much ahead of others of her generation. How did Beverley and Trish get along when they were forced to work very closely with each other? At first the sparks of conflict were rather obvious. But slowly they built a sound working relationship based upon their mutual desire to do a good job for the company and further their careers. They did not become close personal friends, and they did not go out together socially. But they learned to respect each other and both benefited from the working relationship despite their value differences.

It is a mistake, perhaps even an invasion of privacy, to impose one's own personal values on another, especially in the working environment. What a fellow worker does with her private life is her own business and should have nothing to do with the relationship you build with her on the job. To react to an individual in a negative way for what she does on the outside should be avoided. Common interests on the job can always be found upon which to build a good working relationship. You will be surprised how many good working relationships you can build with people who think and live differently than you do.

Mutual reward theory: With proper care, working relationships can turn out to be mutually rewarding and both parties can come out ahead. In fact, if a working relationship is to remain healthy over a long time, it must contribute something of value to both persons. When one individual suddenly discovers that she (or he) has been contributing substantially more than she has been receiving, the relationship can quickly weaken. However, when there is an equal give-and-take between people, the working relationship can thrive. The case of Gabriella illustrates this theory.

Gabriella was a quiet, timid, serious worker with outstanding job knowledge. Joseph, on the other hand, was a very outgoing person with great personal confidence but with less job knowledge. They worked next to each other in identical jobs and, despite their differences, they slowly built a strong relationship.

How did it happen? Gabriella made a patient effort to teach Joseph as much as possible about the job and took care of some mistakes he made without the supervisor finding out about them. What did Joseph do in return? He helped Gabriella develop more self-confidence and become a more outgoing personality. He did this by paying her deserved compliments, introducing her to co-workers from other departments, and generally giving her a feeling of "acceptance" that she had not been able to develop by herself. Because both parties contributed to the success of the other (both eventually became supervisors), their relationship became strong and permanent.

Molly worked for Ms. Gonzales three years before taking over her job as department manager. During that period the mutual-reward theory was constantly in effect. Molly provided high productivity, loyalty, and dependability to the dpeartment and to Ms. Gonzales. Ms. Gonzales, as supervisor, provided a good learning environment for Molly and gave her the recognition she needed. For example, Ms. Gonzales would often introduce Molly to upper-management people and relate the progress she was making. This exposure eventually gave Molly the edge she needed to be chosen as Ms. Gonzales's replacement.

Relationships can almost always be mutually rewarding because people can strengthen each other in many different ways. Obviously, however, when one person does all the giving, deterioration quickly sets in. As you build new relationships and protect old ones, look for things you can do to contribute to the success and happiness of the person next to you. When you do this you will almost always receive something in return that will make life better for you.

Age differences: The new employee who is young, capable, and ambitious is faced with a peculiar challenge in most organizations. And it doesn't take long for the challenge to present itself. You hear it expressed in many ways:

"I could have had that last promotion if I had had more seniority."

"Everyone in this outfit has age, seniority, or experience beyond mine. I'll never get a chance."

"I'm wasting my time and ability. I won't get a chance to show what I can do until I'm thirty."

"I think I'll grow a mustache, so that I'll at least appear older."

Many employees between the ages of eighteen and thirty consider their youth a handicap. Some feel that they must put in time to reach a certain age level before they will be given a chance to demonstrate their ability. In a few cases the situation becomes aggravated because the employee appears younger than he or she actually is.

It is easy to appreciate this attitude if you put yourself in the place of a young employee. He sees older, more experienced employees all around him. He may begin to feel the generation gap is wider inside a business organization than outside. Yet he wants to make progress. He wants to move. He doesn't want to wait. So the pressure builds.

It is not unusual today to find young supervisors in charge of employees many years their senior. Take Laurel and Leonard as examples.

Laurel manages a large fashion department in a major department store. The department had sales of over $400,000 last year. Laurel supervises nine full-time people, all of whom are at least twice her age, which is twenty. The problems are constant and the pressure is great. But, without exception, the older workers consider her an excellent manager and her boss feels she has a great future.

Leonard, who is just twenty-three and has only one year of college behind him, is the manager of a large, popular restaurant. Two of the three managers who work under him are much older than he, and one is old enough to be his father. As a matter of fact, most of the regular employees are older. The establishment is open twenty-four hours a day, and the problems never end. Yet Leonard seems to be on top of everything, and the president of the chain feels that he is just getting started.

How do young people like Laurel and Leonard do it?

They demonstrate early that they can accept and handle responsibility. They demonstrate that they can make mature decisions. They demonstrate great personal confidence. They demonstrate a talent for human relations. They show that they can build strong relationships with older and more experienced employees and management personnel as well as with people their own age. The fact is that your more mature fellow workers will not resist your personal progress if you go about it the right way. Rather, they will want you to succeed and will be willing to help you.

Your decision, then, is a simple one. If you are young and ambitious, you can either drift along until you are older and have more experience, or you can face the human-relations problem now and speed up your progress.

If you decide to make the effort, there are a few important points to remember about building a relationship with an older, more experienced person.

Everyone, regardless of age, likes to be noticed. This is especially true of older employees. They like to receive compliments (even if the compliments border on flattery). They like to feel that they are still important as employees and as people. They need to feel appreciated and respected.

It is a matter of status to be successful and make progress on the job. For an older employee, to be passed up in favor of a younger person is difficult to take. Small wonder that the older, more experienced person may feel threatened by the younger man or woman who is moving up in the organization.

The more mature person often likes to keep a young image. Any action that tends to make this person feel out-of-touch or out-of-date is a mistake. Try to make him (or her) feel that he still has a lot to offer, that he is part of today's world, not yesterday's. Make a big effort to keep the communication lines open at all times. Do not isolate yourself from this person. Always include him in on fun and other activities. Remember, you cannot expect a good vertical relationship with him—should you become his supervisor later on—unless you build a good horizontal working relationship with him now.

Perhaps the most important aspect of building good relationships with mature fellow employees is learning how to gain their respect. This is done through ability, hard work, and reliability on a day-to-day basis.

There is no short, easy route. Deeds will do more than words. Statistics will do more than promises. Performance will do more than flattery.

Friendliness and personal interest are certainly important. But performance is the most important element in building a sound relationship with an older co-worker.

More than anything else, *learn* from this person. Her (or his) additional years of experience have taught her many things that you can learn without having to experience them. You can learn through osmosis. Consider yourself an apprentice and learn. Then, if the time comes for you to move ahead of her, give her credit for making it possible. Let her have the satisfaction of calling you her protégée. Let her take pride in your success.

It will be wise of you to accept her role as an expert in areas where she is obviously better qualified than you.

It will be wise of you to keep your relationship on a formal basis until she gives you the signal to be more relaxed and personal.

What about reversing the situation? How can the mature worker build better relationships with the new, younger employee? There are many steps that can be taken. Here are three that will be greatly appreciated: (1) be patient with new employees' adjustment problems, (2) help them learn by sharing your experience with them, and (3) if needed, give them the confidence to communicate with you.

Irritation threshold: Relationships are frequently endangered because one of the individuals has an irritating habit or mannerism that bothers the other. Here are some common ones:

> Harsh, overbearing voices
> Irritating laughs
> Constant name dropping
> Constant talk about money
> Constant reference to sex
> Telling dirty or unfunny stories
> Overuse of certain words or expressions
> Constant discussion of personal problems
> Constant complaining
> Constant bragging about success

Whether or not a habit or mannerism becomes an irritant depends upon the threshold or *tolerance level* of the second party. If one party has a high enough threshold he or she may not even notice an irritant that might bother someone else. On the other hand, it is possible for an individual to have a very low threshold to a certain mannerism, in which case the habit can do considerable damage to the relationship.

Diane is an excellent example of a young employee who hurt her relationship with a few fellow workers because of a nervous giggle that followed almost every sentence she uttered. Unfortunately, Diane had no idea what was happening. She was not conscious of the habit or of the fact that it was hurting her relationships with certain people who had low thresholds. One day, after getting a complaint from a good employee who worked next to Diane, the supervisor had a talk with her about it and, thanks to some very hard work on Diane's part, the irritating mannerism all but disappeared in a few weeks.

Once the individual knows about them, bad habits can usually be modified and sometimes eliminated. But the person at the other end of the relationship must not expect too much too soon. In some cases it may be necessary to learn to live with certain irritants by making an attempt to raise one's tolerance level. Seldom do such irritants come from only one side of the relationship. Almost all of us have at least a few mannerisms or habits that bother other people. The individual, even in the business environment, retains the right to remain pretty much the way he or she is, so some adjustment on your part to such factors will be necessary in most relationships.

Ethnic implications: A basic human-relations principle is to respect and treat every person as a unique and special individual. Look beyond outward appearances, ignore how he or she might resemble someone you have had an unfavorable experience with in the past, and accept each person for himself alone. If everybody could sincerely adhere to this one fundamental practice, relationships would have a good chance of functioning harmoniously. Each person—and each relationship—would stand on its own without reference to ethnic background. Unfortunately for all of us, not enough people practice this principle. Here are two short cases to illustrate the point.

Although she had always believed she was free of prejudice, Jean had had very little close contact with blacks. She was therefore a little uneasy about working closely with a black person for the first time. Hobart, a young black, joined the department and, after introductions, Jean's uneasiness gave way to anticipation. Hobart was a very easygoing, friendly guy. He would be fun to work with.

Everything went very well as far as their relationship was concerned until Hobart started to make a number of mistakes. He kept asking what Jean felt were stupid questions and, in general, he did not live up to her expectations. Jean became so frustrated over the matter that she was tempted to go to her supervisor.

Then, all of a sudden, it came to her that she was expecting more of Hobart because he was black. She was looking for things to complain about instead of being understanding like she would normally be with a white person. Jean decided to get the relationship back on a fair footing, so she invited Hobart for coffee and admitted her mistake. It was a good move because Hobart had felt Jean's negative attitude and wanted to build a better relationship himself.

Fernando and Archie were assigned two months ago to work as a team on a moving van. Archie had graduated from a community college and hoped eventually to get into management. Fernando, a very sensitive Chicano, was a high school dropout with over three years' experience in the furniture-moving business.

Archie learned quickly that Fernando was an outstanding worker with excellent skills. He also learned in a hurry that Fernando was not much of a talker. In fact, Fernando only communicated when it was necessary to get the job done.

This silence soon got on Archie's nerves. After making many attempts to get a light conversation going, he decided that Fernando had a lot of deep-seated hostility toward Anglos. It was a very uncomfortable situation, and because Archie needed to talk, he soon became a little bitter about the situation. Should he ask for a transfer? Should he resign?

Then one day it occurred to him that, with a few beers, Fernando might open up and they could learn to communicate. He invited Fernando to be his guest, and they went to a place close to Fernando's home. It was a small place that reflected the Chicano culture. Sure enough, it wasn't long before Fernando felt sufficiently comfortable to start talking.

Archie learned a great deal. Fernando had been pushed around by many people. He did not feel accepted. His silence was more a defense than anything else. But what got to Archie was the fact that Fernando felt that Archie was against *him*, and not the other way around.

It was a revelation for both parties, and much of the tension that was present on the job previously was gone the next day. Archie and Fernando learned how to communicate. As a result, they started to work much better as a team. They didn't become personal friends, but they gained a high degree of mutual toleration.

There are many relationships ahead of you that will have certain ethnic implications. They will not always be easy to understand. Sometimes they may demand more perception than you possess. Yet, if you are open, honest, sincere, and willing to talk, your chances of building sound relationships are excellent.

Sexual overtones: Working relationships between men and women almost always have sexual overtones. For the most part, this sexual tension is not dangerous and has little important influence one way or the other on productivity.

If you are a man, you will develop a different kind of relationship with a woman than you would with another man. For example, if your supervisor is a woman, you should be careful not to let your male ego prevent you from seeing that many women make excellent managers.

If you are a woman, you will develop a different kind of relationship with a man than you would with another woman. For example, if your male supervisor or a fellow employee regularly makes plays for you, you should be polite but firm in maintaining a business-only relationship.

The great majority of men and women work together without any serious complications arising because of sex. The overtones remain subdued and have no adverse influence on productivity. But not always. Take the case of Judy.

Judy was attracted sexually to her supervisor from the moment he was transferred into her department. A perceptive observer would have noticed that the very next day she started wearing the best clothes in her wardrobe. She became more particular with her makeup. She started working harder to win the favor of her new boss and to create more opportunities to talk with him on business matters.

So what happened? The other women in Judy's department

quickly sensed the sexual overtones to the relationship and their attitude toward Judy began to cool off. They became more distant, less willing to help her, and less tolerant of her mistakes. It didn't take long for a certain strain to develop among all employees in the department, and productivity began to suffer.

Judy's case raises a very difficult question: *What are the human-relations dangers involved in dating someone where you work?*

There is little danger involved providing the individual is not your supervisor, he or she works in a section separated from yours, and you are smart enough to keep your business and personal worlds apart. Under these circumstances, management will probably be very understanding. After all, it is only normal and healthy for people of the opposite sex to be attracted to one another. Management cannot keep this from happening.

There are some real dangers, however, that you should know about in advance. Most of them occur under the following circumstances: (1) when a supervisor dates someone in his or her own department, thus raising immediate cries of favoritism and hurting productivity; (2) when two people—especially if they are in the same section—date and do not keep their business and personal worlds separate, thus hurting relationships with others and eventually lowering productivity, and (3) when one or both parties are married, thus creating a sticky situation that can produce harmful gossip, hurt productivity, and sometimes make it necessary for management to step in.

Before you create or accept a dating situation where you work, you should also consider the chance of a breakup between the two of you at a later date. This could hurt both people involved and leave hard feelings among fellow employees who were in on the matter and took sides.

Another point to keep in mind is the action you would take should the dating become serious and marriage plans evolve. In cases of this nature, it would be a good human-relations move on your part to announce the decision to management personally, before they find out about it secondhand. Management appreciates receiving such important information directly, and within the framework of written policy, they can sometimes be very accommodating.

The "hurt syndrome": There is a real danger that in building a worthwhile working relationship you might get your feelings hurt. All relationships are built on an emotional foundation. This being the case, people may expect more from a working relationship than is reasonable, and consequently may wind up getting hurt. Here is a simple illustration of the point.

Mary and Sally joined the company the same day, and because they were thrown together during the orientation period, they became very close. For the first few weeks they spent all of their breaks together, isolated themselves from others during lunch, and became increasingly dependent upon each other.

Unfortunately, Mary became overdependent, and when Sally suddenly made a move to build relationships with others, Mary felt rejected and hurt. It put a big strain on the working relationship for a few days. Then Sally, sensing Mary's reaction, initiated a long conversation about the matter. When Mary understood that Sally felt it was good human relations to build other relationships, and that she had not been snubbed, Mary felt better and decided to build some new working relationships herself.

Do those individuals who concentrate on building strong and healthy working relationships frequently live through a painful incident of some kind? The answer is yes. Many people make the mistake of trying to satisfy personal needs from a working relationship, when only a personal or social relationship can do it. In short, they expect too much from working relationships.

Of course, it is difficult to build any relationship without occasional feelings of disappointment. We frequently expect more from the individual at the other end of the relationship than we should. Even those professionals who are highly successful at human relations must live through a few hurt feelings without magnifying them beyond their real dimensions. They must avoid pushing their disappointments with people underground where they fester and become distorted.

Instead, they should discard them and continue to look for the healthy parts of the relationship. They must refuse to let the "hurt syndrome" destroy relationships that are basically sound and should be maintained.

As we conclude this chapter, there should be little doubt in the reader's mind about one thing: job relationships are intriguing, unpredictable, sometimes sticky, and—unlike personal and social relationships—are not freely chosen. They are sometimes hard to build in the first place, and they need constant attention to keep them healthy. Yet, despite all of this, they are fascinating and rewarding. As you move into the world of work on a career basis, you will have more and more opportunities to build strong and satisfying working relationships at all levels with all kinds of people.

PROBLEM 8
Communication

Maria was an intelligent, sensitive college sophomore who worked part-time with a local banking organization. She hoped to move into a good full-time career with the same company upon graduation in June.

Although she was fairly successful in her part-time job because she was accurate, reliable, and conscientious, Maria did not communicate well with her fellow workers. If she met a new girl on campus and the relationship began to get a little personal, she cut it off. When one of her fellow workers tried to be friendly, she was polite, but backed away. When someone tried to involve her in a discussion by asking a question, Maria came up with a quick answer but made no effort to keep the conversation going.

Maria's supervisor, an individual with many years of experience said, "I have talked with her a number of times, and I still can't understand her. She is a good producer but she seems to be afraid to put even a little of herself into a relationship.

"I used to think it was just a matter of being shy and timid, but I am not so sure anymore. She seems to prefer being alone. It seems painful for her to communicate. Sometimes I sense a little hostility or defiance in her manner. Has she been hurt in the past? Is there something about her Chicano culture I don't understand? Am I a threat to her? Is it the age difference between her and her co-workers?

"At any rate, she doesn't seem to recognize that *she* has a responsibility to communicate. Until she learns this I am not going to recommend her for a full-time position, because it would not be fair to her fellow workers and to her future career success."

If you were Maria's supervisor, how would you go about helping her to learn to communicate? (For suggested answer, see page 192.)

9

Thirteen Tips on Succeeding in a New Job or Assignment

Undoubtedly you want to be successful on a new job or assignment. First, you want to prove to your family, friends, and management that you are capable. Second, you want to prove it to yourself. There is a great deal at stake.

This chapter is devoted to thirteen tips that can be of great help to you in reaching this goal. If you take these tips seriously, you will avoid many of the mistakes others make.

Tip 1: Take a calendar notebook to work with you.

An abundance of important information, rules, regulations, and procedures will be thrown at you in the beginning. The first days

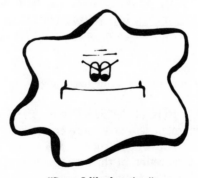

"Sure, I like hot tips."

are days of adjustment and excitement, so don't trust your mind to remember everything. Rather, buy yourself an inexpensive calendar notebook and use it to record some of the instructions and hard-to-remember information you get from your supervisor or fellow workers. Jot this data down in your notebook. Don't be afraid to do this while the person giving it to you is talking or watching.

The notebook itself (if not overused) will create a good impression. It will help show that you are an organized person and are methodical in your approach to learning. In the evening, it can be used to review certain facts and procedures. It can also be used to record appointments, ideas, names, and so on.

Tip 2: Safeguard your means of transportation.

It is your responsibility to be at work on time. One of the worst things you can do is to report late during your first few weeks —or anytime, for that matter.

If you depend on public transportation, be sure to check the schedule carefully and give yourself plenty of time to make connections. It is much better to be thirty minutes early than three minutes late. If you have your own automobile, be sure you keep it in good mechanical order. Check the tires frequently. Be sure you have sufficient gas. Have some preventive maintenance done to protect yourself. Also, allow yourself extra driving time.

If you depend on someone else for transportation, be sure he (or she) is a dependable person who feels the same way you do about getting to work on time. If you feel he is not dependable, make other arrangements. It is your responsibility to get to work on time. *Management will not be interested in your excuses.*

Tip 3: Conserve your energy at the beginning.

The strain and tension of the first few days and weeks on your new job or assignment will take more energy out of your system than you expect. You will frequently feel drained at the end of the day. As an illustration of this, it is quite common for a new employee to catch a cold and miss a day or two of work during her (or his) first weeks of employment. To prevent this from happening to you, conserve your energy until you make the adjustment. Don't commit yourself to a heavy social schedule or to long weekend trips. Avoid keeping excessively late hours. You need to be especially alert during your first few weeks of employment, so be sure to get plenty of sleep.

Tip 4: Ask questions, but learn to ask the right ones.

If you don't understand something, ask questions until you do. This may be necessary because those responsible for your training do not always take enough time to explain things fully. They forget that they often talk too fast and that it is sometimes impossible for you to get the full message the first time around.

In such a situation, it is better to ask for a replay so that you will not make the same mistake over and over again. Fear of being considered stupid is the reason most people do not ask more questions. This is understandable, but it is better to ask questions than to suffer the serious results of continued mistakes.

There is a right and wrong time to ask a question. One should not, for example, interrupt a person who is concentrating on getting a job done or who is communicating with others. Wait for a more convenient time to ask your question.

Tip 5: Use good judgment in working extra hours and taking your breaks.

Some new employees attempt to secure their jobs and attract management's attention by working more than the normal number of hours at the beginning. They arrive first in the morning and make a point of leaving last at the end of the day. They often skip their breaks. This attitude, if sincere, is to be admired.

However, overzealousness can get you into trouble on two counts. First, there are usually regulations governing hours to be worked. On certain jobs, unauthorized overtime work and failure to take breaks can involve you and your employer in labor difficulties. It is important, therefore, always to abide by the instructions given to you by management.

Second, your fellow employees may misinterpret your motives and make life more difficult for you and your supervisor. Working extra hours and eliminating breaks when an important deadline must be met and when you are asked to do it by your supervisor is one thing. Working extra hours only to impress others is quite another.

As a rule, it is better to make full use of the time you spend on the job than to try to impress others with your willingness to work extra hours.

Tip 6: Don't flaunt your education and intelligence.

It is possible that you will have more formal education than many of the people you will work with on your new job. But these people probably have far more on-the-job experience and practical know-how than you do. That being the case, you would be wise to let them discover your educational background gradually.

You are entitled to be proud of your educational achievements, but you will probably get off to a better start if you don't broadcast the fact. The job you are assigned may be more difficult than you expect. If you try to impress people with your education or intelligence, they may not want to give you any help when you most need it.

You may have learned how to do a job in a particular way. You will probably find at your new job that things are done differently. Perhaps your way of doing things is better. But until you are *sure*, be safe and do it the way the people at your new job do it. Give the experienced person the satisfaction of explaining how to do things *his* (or her) way. This will also give you a chance to build good relationships with your fellow workers. It will be to your advantage in the long run. You will have plenty of time later to use your intelligence and apply your education.

Tip 7: Make friends, but don't make close friends too soon.

There are many little human-relations traps you can easily fall into during your first days on a new job. One of these is building one or two very strong friendships at the expense of all others. For example, suppose you discover that one of the employees in your department is extremely friendly the first day. Such friendliness is usually more than welcome the first few hours in a strange setting.

But beware. What if you spend all your time with this one employee and neglect being friendly to the others? What if this friendly person is not respected by the others? What if he or she has earned a poor reputation in the department and is offering you friendship from purely selfish motives?

Sometimes people who have failed to earn respect from others at work try desperately to win the friendship of a new employee. Remember that it is only natural that the employees (including management) will quickly identify you with any employee or employees you spend excessive time with.

If one employee clings to you as you start your new job, you obviously have a difficult situation to handle. Of course, you should not be rude to this person. You will do well, however, to back away and be somewhat reserved toward this individual for the first few weeks and concentrate on building relationships with *all* people rather than just one.

Tip 8: Look energetic, but don't be an eager beaver.

Some young people start their careers with a great burst of energy and enthusiasm that cannot possibly be sustained. These people frequently create a favorable impression to begin with, but later on they are reclassified by both management and their fellow workers.

It is easy to be overeager at the beginning. You are new to your job, so you have a fresh and dynamic approach. You have a great deal of nervous energy to release. You are interested, and your interest motivates you to achieve. This desire to succeed, however, might cause you to reach too far too fast.

The best way to make progress inside an organization is to make *steady* progress. If you set an unusually fast pace you will have a hard time keeping it up. Furthermore, if you concentrate too hard on getting the job done, you might neglect the people with whom you are working. You will have plenty of time to demonstrate high personal productivity later. But if you move too fast at the start, you could make some serious human-relations mistakes that might hurt you in the future.

Tip 9: Different organizations have different personal-appearance and grooming standards.

A few organizations, like factories, have no personal-appearance or grooming standards. They are interested only in your work performance and your human-relations ability. What you look like doesn't matter, because only your fellow workers see you.

Other companies, especially those which directly serve customers, set minimum standards that are usually easy to live up to. Still other companies, like department stores, have rather high personal and grooming standards that may be difficult for some people to accept.

When you join an organization you should carefully assess the situation and decide what is best for you and your future. You have a right to be yourself and to protect your individuality. In doing so, however, you should weigh all factors and take into consideration that most people, including management, feel that a little conformity won't hurt you.

Tip 10: Read your employee handbook and other materials carefully.

Many organizations publish handbooks and other materials for new employees. These pamphlets usually contain vital information. Yet many new employees never read them.

Don't be casual in your use of company literature. Where else can you learn company policies that can keep you out of trouble? Where else can you discover important data that will prevent you from asking unnecessary questions? Take home all of the literature you are given and devote some time to it. Understanding your company better will help you start on the right foot.

Tip 11: Be yourself, but be your best self.

Make your best effort to create a good first impression, but be natural about it. You must accept and be satisfied with yourself as you are and not try to copy others. Phony mannerisms will defeat your purpose.

You can admire another person, but you cannot be that person.

You can envy another personality, but you cannot have that personality. You can aspire to a reputation for good grooming that another person enjoys, but that does not mean that you must dress like that person. If you attempt to copy others, you risk destroying the better facets of your own personality. Just be yourself—your best self.

Tip 12: Listen with your eyes as well as your ears.

In face-to-face conversations, you must listen as much with your eyes as with your ears. Sure, you receive the auditory impressions through your ears. But you give the person speaking your attention with your eyes. Some people feel it is discourteous to let your eyes wander when they are talking to you. You will understand this if you have ever seen someone look at his watch, stare at the floor, or look out a window while you are talking to him. You will make a better impression on people if you form the habit of listening with your eyes as well as your ears.

Tip 13: Send out some positive signals.

A friendly person—one who creates a good first impression—is one who uses certain positive signals when she (or he) meets others. She takes the initiative. She makes the first effort. For example, a person with a ready smile is easily interpreted as a friendly person. The smile seems to break any psychological barriers that might exist in a meeting of strangers. You immediately feel accepted by this person. The smile, then, is a friendly signal.

There are many other signals one can use to create a good first impression. "Hello," "Good morning," and "Thank you" are examples of friendly verbal signals. Such easy signals of friendship should be transmitted at every opportunity to acknowledge the presence of others and to recognize any courtesies they have extended to you, however small.

There are also many effective nonverbal signals in addition to the smile. Shaking hands, gesturing positively with the hand or head, opening doors for people—these are all signals you send that make it easier for people to meet and know you. When you send out such signals naturally and in good taste, others do not feel awkward about approaching you. You have made it easy for them, and they like you for it.

People who develop confidence in sending out such signals of friendship make excellent first impressions. They quickly increase their sphere of influence and build many lasting working and personal relationships. Have confidence in yourself and your ability to send such signals. Take the initiative. Send out your own brand of signals in your own style, and be an easier person to meet. You will be pleased with the results.

Remember, too, that the better you become at this the better prepared you will be for any job interviews you may be faced with in the future. Good human relations is really good common sense.

PROBLEM 9
Eagerness

Ed was considered by his close friends to be something of a con artist. He had an overabundance of energy. In college, he was always involved in a wide variety of campus activities. Whenever he was in a group he was rather loud and aggressive. Those who knew him best considered him to be extremely competitive. Ed himself admitted that he was a poor loser.

After graduating from college, Ed went to work in the marketing department of a large, progressive company. He wanted to prove himself quickly, and started out like a ball of fire. He expressed himself freely in staff meetings, quickly learned the names of all co-workers and managers, and engaged those in upper-management positions in frequent conversations.

Ed had made up his mind not to leave a single human-relations rock unturned. In fact, just a few weeks after he started, the word had gotten around management circles that he was a real eager beaver and was destined for greater things inside the company.

What degree of success would you predict for Ed? What are the advantages and the dangers of his approach? What human-relations mistakes might he be making? (For a suggested answer, see page 193.)

10

The First Weeks
Are Critical

It used to be that most organizations offered a few days or more of classroom orientation for all new employees. Those destined for management were often put through many months of nonproductive training before being given their first responsible work assignment. For the most part, however, those days are over.

Today the vast majority of firms expect and receive almost immediate productivity from the new employee. Most training takes place on the job. Here is the way a corporate training director expresses the change:

"In the past when things in general were more stable and employee turnover in particular was less frequent, we could afford to take more time to train new employees before giving them work assignments. For example, we could take a few days to dis-

"Hank's O.K. . . . he just needs motivation."

cuss the history of the company and explain policies and procedures.

"We just don't have the time or the budget for that anymore, primarily because we have such a high turnover rate. We now must work to get the new employee productive as soon as possible, often the first day he or she comes to work. This means two things. First, it means that most of our training must take place on the work site.

Second, it means that the employee must learn about company policies and procedures from reading employee manuals. Most of our new employees seem to like it this way, however, especially those who qualify for management training programs. Apparently they feel they have spent enough time in the classroom.

" 'Shape up or ship out' is an old Navy expression that has a special meaning when you join an organization and may be on a temporary or probationary status. It means 'adjust quickly to the requirements of your new job or you might get off on the wrong foot, hurt your future, or even get fired.' "

It is not the purpose of this chapter to make you uneasy about your first new job. Rather it is designed to help you understand just what "early productivity" and "probationary status" mean. In the past, many unsuspecting new employees discovered the true meaning of these factors too late.

There is nothing new about probationary periods in business and industry. All beginning employees have a probationary period. It is traditional. It gives management a last chance to evaluate a person before granting permanent status. It is, in effect, the final screening device in the selection program of a company. You have been interviewed, hired, and given the green light on a temporary basis. But before you are accepted as a permanent employee, management must make quite sure they haven't made a mistake.

They have their reasons.

Permanent status is a big thing. It isn't something most companies hand out easily. With permanent status come many things not usually given to temporary employees—vacation benefits, seniority privileges, and profit-sharing, to mention a few. In some organizations it takes years to achieve permanent status.

For example, you may qualify for a civil-service position with the United States government by passing certain oral and written tests. You would then be placed on an eligibility list. If you are at the top of the list and qualify for a position that is open, you may receive a job. Does this mean that you have permanent status? Far from it! In fact, you may be on a temporary status for years before you receive a permanent civil-service appointment.

Why? Because once you achieve permanent status under the Civil Service Act, you receive many additional advantages. You cannot be terminated except under certain circumstances and through specified procedures. You have certain transfer priorities. You have seniority for certain promotions. You have protection against layoffs. Permanent status with civil service is something to work for over a period of years. It is not easily achieved.

Although most business and industrial organizations usually have much less complicated procedures, the same principle applies. Permanent status does not always come automatically.

This is also true for most crafts. A young person starts out as an apprentice and works slowly to become a journeyman. He (or she) must perform successfully on the job and in the classroom for two to four years before he can become a journeyman. He does not have permanent status until he reaches this goal. Once he receives his certificate, however, he is a recognized journeyman under state law and is given certain privileges and opportunities.

Probationary periods, of course, differ from organization to organization. In some companies it is only a week or possibly thirty days. If you survive, you are considered permanent. Other organizations have probationary periods of two, three, or six months. In some companies it takes a full year to achieve permanent status.

Some organizations are very formal about their probationary periods. Others are very informal. Some have none at all. If your company has clearly spelled out your probationary period, you know where you stand. If it has not, it would be a smart move on your part to inquire. Don't be fooled about the probationary period just because no one has specifically talked to you about it. Find out for sure. In a month or two it may be too late.

Permanent status does not mean 100 percent job security, but in most cases it is a big step in that direction. Permanent status means a great deal in organizations that have a "promotion from within" philosophy. Many companies make a real effort to employ only those people who are promotable to higher positions. They want to promote from within their own organization. Except in unusual cases, they refrain from employing outsiders for anything except starting or entry jobs. Naturally, a company with this practice would hesitate to give permanent status to someone who could not grow with the company over the years.

There are two conditions of your probationary status that you should consider in advance.

First, your time may be limited. You may have only a short while to demonstrate your capabilities. Once the time is up, the company must decide whether to keep you or not. So make the most of your time. Don't let it slip by without making your very best effort.

Second, you must change a few habits. Look at it this way. Perhaps you have just spent twelve to sixteen years in school. Or you have just resigned a position with a company with different practices and procedures. Or you have been out of the labor market for some time and are unaccustomed to the discipline of work. Whatever the case, chances are you have formed many habits from your previous experiences or routines. Some of these habits are deeply set. Now, within a few days, *you are expected to change your habits*. The rules may be different. The requirements are different. The procedures are not the same. You must either shape up or ship out.

Can you change your habits? And can you change them in time? Here are a few examples of new employees who failed.

1. Betsy received a substantial raise when she moved from one banking organization to another. With ten years of experience in methods of procedures behind her, she had a lot to offer the new company. Betsy ran into trouble, however, because she could not adjust. Instead of accepting the new policies and procedures, she constantly compared them with her old company's and tried to change some of them. Her constant reference to how things were done at her old company did not set well. Betsy was terminated in less than a year.

2. Sue was very popular in school. She had many friends and seldom missed a social event of any kind. The same was true on her first job. Everybody stopped to talk with her, and time went

so fast on her breaks that she was often late returning to her desk. Sue didn't realize that excessive socializing was not acceptable in business. She had to lose her first job to learn that.

3. When Gil finished college, he decided he wanted to live a little. He bought a new car, shared a fancy apartment with a high-living friend, and started a promising career with a large company. Gil didn't exactly keep regular hours. Soon this began to have an effect on him and his work. Gil kept his job for just three months before he was released.

Habits that have taken years to form are not easily changed. Poor habits must often be replaced with good habits during an adjustment period. Habits that were acceptable in one situation might have to be replaced with habits that are acceptable in another situation. The truth is that business and industrial organizations expect you to make a quick and satisfactory adjustment to *their* way of doing things.

Most young people accept their first job with an organization on an exploratory basis. In other words, they don't make a firm commitment to themselves to stay with the company until they have had a good chance to respond to the work environment, the work itself, management attitudes, and many other factors. This is a natural attitude, and it is expected and understood by most personnel people. Experience has taught them to anticipate serious misgivings on the part of new employees. Many employees will wonder: "Do I really belong here?" "Is this what I really want?" "Did I look far enough before accepting this opportunity?"

If the misgivings are permanent, the employee should seek work elsewhere. Usually, however, the uncertainty that many new employees experience during their first few months is just a symptom of a transition period. Some employees become temporarily discouraged because of the unexpected discipline their new job demands. Others become frustrated over problems they did not anticipate and were not trained to cope with. Still others become disappointed with the routine of the work or the treatment they receive from their supervisor. Most employees make the necessary adjustments easily and live through them without any great trauma. Others have more trouble. Take Hank for example.

Hank was a very impatient, verbal, aggressive, and energetic guy who had to be around people to be happy. It seemed quite natural when he accepted a job with a big retailer. There, people would appreciate his personality and give him responsibility in a hurry. He started out on the company's training program with great enthusiasm. Things went very well for a few weeks.

Gradually, however, Hank had to face up to the odd working hours that are traditional in the retail business, the great amount of detailed paper work that he didn't anticipate, and a heavy load of problems that required immediate decisions. It all got to Hank after about two months, and he was all set to turn in his resignation.

Luckily, however, Hank's supervisor sensed his dilemma and guided him through the awkward period. He explained the advantages of the odd hours by discussing his own life-style to a limited extent. He taught Hank how to handle detailed paperwork faster and talked him into taking a speed-reading course. He gave him tips on decision making and on setting priorities.

Three years later Hank was happy and successful. He was certain he had found the right career and the right company. Of course, he also realized that he was lucky to have had a perceptive supervisor.

The following suggestions will be helpful should you, too, become disenchanted with your new job.

1. *Anticipate a few bad days or even weeks.* This may not happen, but it's natural for most employees to have some misgivings about their first job choice. If it happens, realize that it is a normal pattern and that chances are good you will live through it without any serious problems at all.

2. *Give yourself plenty of time.* You will need to give yourself ample time to fully explore and adjust to the opportunity you have accepted, so don't panic the first time something goes wrong. Some experts feel that you should give yourself a full year on a job so that an early negative reaction does not cause a premature resignation. Just remember that most new employees live through touchy periods. Give yourself all the time you need to make a complete personal adjustment. See the overall picture instead of just the immediate problems.

3. *Try to keep a negative attitude from showing.* If you are not careful, you will let your transition problems give you a negative

attitude that will be hard to hide, especially from management. If you let a negative attitude become apparent, you could injure relationships that will be difficult to repair later on.

It would be wise to talk your adjustment problem over with your supervisor. However, it is usually best not to discuss such problems with your fellow employees. They may be unhappy themselves and thus reinforce your negative attitude. They could indirectly cause you to make a decision you might regret later.

What should you do if you discover that your skills are not up to the demands of your new job? The best thing to do, of course, is to find a way to upgrade them during your off-hours so that your on-the-job progress will not be curtailed. This might mean going back to school at night or taking some special training. Most new employees who discover the need to improve their skills are able to do something about it.

Many organizations have a thirty- or sixty-day appraisal. This may or may not be tied to a probationary program. At any rate, it is extremely important. If you can make better than average progress *before* your first appraisal, however, you should get a good report and be off to an excellent start. This should reinforce your confidence in your job performance.

But be careful. One new employee in a large banking institution recently had this to say: "I was so pleased with my first formal appraisal and the fact that I survived the probationary period that I relaxed too much. With the help of some informal counseling, however, my supervisor finally got me back on an up attitude."

PROBLEM 10
Supervisor

Sandy was unemployed for almost a year before winning a job with an outstanding company three months ago. It was not long before she felt she had a serious, perhaps unsolvable, problem with her immediate supervisor Mr. Shark. She recently related the matter to her close friend Hazel. "I just can't believe this is happening to me. He is driving me up the wall. He is overdemanding and I sense some real inner hostility against me. I have not in any way crossed him, undermined him, or conducted myself in such a way that I would be a threat to him or his role as a supervisor. He is bad enough in his treatment of the other employees in our department, but he is unreal in his treatment of me. I have been so upset that I have stayed home three times in the last two weeks."

Last night, with Hazel's assistance, they listed the following options for Sandy.

1. Resign and take a trip to Hawaii. Sandy could borrow the money and then start out fresh upon her return.

2. Confront Mr. Shark. Demand an appointment and have it out. No holds barred. If Sandy is terminated she can get a lawyer to bring suit against the company for unfair practices.

3. Go over Mr. Shark's head and "blow the whistle loud and clear." In such a meeting both Mr. Shark's boss and the director of personnel would be asked to be present.

4. Last him out. Refuse to knuckle under. Stand her ground, keep her productivity up, build good human relationships with others, and eventually take Mr. Shark's job away from him.

5. Behave in such a manner that Mr. Shark will become so upset with her that he will terminate her services without cause. This will enable Sandy to collect unemployment insurance while she is looking for a better job or sunning in Hawaii.

6. Laugh it off and survive without hostility or rancor. Refuse to let Mr. Shark intimidate her. Just do what the rest of the employees are doing.

Which of the above options, if any, would you suggest for Sandy? What additional information would you want before taking any action? What responsibility, if any, does Sandy have to try and build a sound relationship with Mr. Shark? What might be behind Mr. Shark's unusual behavior toward Sandy? What difference might it make if Sandy had been with the organization for three years instead of only for three months? (For a suggested answer, see page 194.)

11

How to Handle
Teasing and Testing

Getting started in a new job or assignment where the setting is strange and the employees are strangers is bound to give you a few psychological challenges. It is not my purpose to magnify these. Rather, I wish to help you better understand *why* such problems sometimes develop. Even more important, how can you handle them?

Of course management, especially the personnel and training departments, will give you every possible kind of assistance during your first few days and weeks at work. That is their job. But no matter how much they do, chances are that not everyone in the organization will give you an easy time.

You may be assigned to a department as a replacement for someone the others hated to lose. They will need time to get used to you. You may not have the experience of the person you replace, and as a result others may have to work harder for a few

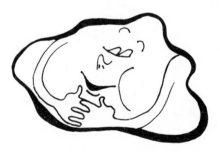

"What are they up to this time?"

days to get you started. It is even possible that someone in your new department wanted another person to have your job, and there may be some resentment toward you because of this.

It is never easy to be the newest member of a group. You cannot expect to go from being an outsider to being an insider without making a few adjustments. In the first place, you and your personality were *forced* upon the group. They were not asked whether they wanted you or, not. You have been, in effect, imposed upon them. Because they were there first, and because they probably have strong relationships among themselves, they may feel that you should earn your way into their confidence. It may not seem fair, but it is only natural for them to look at your arrival in this way.

Did you ever go through an initiation into a club? If so, you will understand that teasing or testing the new member is often traditional. To a limited extent, the same can be true when a new employee joins a department or division in a business organization. There is nothing planned or formal about it, of course, but you should be prepared for a little good-natured teasing or testing. Let us look at the psychological reasons behind these two phenomena.

The teasing of the new employee is often nothing more than a way of helping the person become a full-fledged member of the group. It is a form of initiation rite that will help you feel you belong. Sometimes it is a group effort in which everyone is in on the joke. More often, however, it is an individual matter.

Teasing, for the most part, is harmless.

The shop foreman who has never had the advantage of a college education, but has learned a great deal from practical experience, might enjoy teasing a recent graduate of an engineering school. If the graduate engineer goes along with the teasing, a sound relationship between the two should develop. If, however, she (or he) permits it to get under her skin, the relationship could become strained.

The shop foreman's motive might be nothing more than a desire to help the new engineer build good relationships with the rest of the gang. There may be nothing resentful or personal about it.

A small group of employees who work closely together in a branch bank, lawyers' office, or similar situation can usually be expected to come up with a little harmless teasing when a new person joins the staff. He might be given the oldest typewriter with a touch of formal ceremony or the dismal job of keeping the stockroom in order.

Usually, this kind of teasing is based upon tradition and human nature. People who like to tease in this manner are generally good-natured. They enjoy people. They mean no harm. In fact, they usually do it to make you feel more comfortable, not less.

If you are on the receiving end of some good, healthy teasing, you have nothing to worry about so long as you don't take it personally. Just go along with it and you'll come out ahead. It is much better to be teased than to be ignored. If by chance the baiting should go a little too far and you find yourself embarrassed, the very fact that it is embarrassing to you will probably make you some friends. In fact, you will be lucky if there is some mild hazing. It will help you get off to a good start. It will help break down any communication barriers that might exist.

Testing is different. It can have more serious implications. It will take more understanding on your part.

There are two kinds of testing. One is *organizational testing*. This kind comes from the organization (management, personnel, or your supervisor) and is a deliberate attempt to discover what kind of person you really are and whether or not you can adjust to certain conditions. The other kind comes strictly from individuals. This is *personal testing*—one person trying out another because of personality conflicts or inner prejudices.

Let's look at organizational testing first.

Almost all kinds of organizations—especially the smaller ones —have certain unpleasant tasks that must be done. Traditionally, these tasks are handed to the newest member. The new salesperson in a department store may be given excessive amounts of stock work at the start of his or her career. The factory worker may be given unpleasant cleanup jobs until another new member joins the department. The clerical employee may be given a nasty filing assignment to start with.

Upon leaving college, the author joined a large company that manufactured and distributed ice cream. For the first six weeks he did nothing but stack ice cream in a room where the temperature was below freezing. It was the least desirable assignment in the department and it certainly did not require a college education. After the six-week period, it was possible to look back and see that the assignment was nothing but a planned test. *All* new employees in the department were given this job to start with. It was traditional. It had happened to everyone in the department.

The important thing for the new worker to recognize is that these tests have a purpose. Can the new worker take the assignment without complaining? Can he survive without developing a negative attitude? Or will he show resentment and thereby destroy his chance of gaining the respect of the other members of the department?

The old phrase "starting at the bottom of the ladder" sometimes means exactly that. Many top management people started at the bottom, and they feel that this is the best way for you to start. If you can't take it to begin with, you may not be able to assume heavy responsibility later. It is the price you pay for being a beginner.

Management sometimes feels that this is the best way for the manager of the future to fully appreciate the kind of work that must be done by the rank-and-file employee. Many a college graduate finds herself (or himself) doing the most uninviting tasks to start with. If she is human-relations smart she will take it in stride, using the time to size up the situation and learn as much about the organization as possible.

During testing periods you are being watched by management and your fellow employees. *The better you react, the sooner the testing will end and the better your relations with others will be.* In other words, although getting the job done is important, your attitude toward it may be more important. If you react in a negative manner, three things can happen: (1) you may be kept on the assignment longer than you otherwise would have been, (2) you may hurt your chances for a better assignment later on, and (3) you may damage relationships with those people involved in or observing the testing.

If you can take the long-range perspective and condition yourself to do these tasks with an inner smile and on outward grin, you'll do well for yourself. Roll up your sleeves and get the job done quickly. If you finish one job, move on to another. Don't be afraid to get dirty. If you must take a little abuse, don't complain. It is part of the initiation rite, and you will look back on it someday as those ahead of you look back on it now. It would be foolhardy for the new employee to fight any of the many forms of organizational testing as long as it doesn't seriously damage his or her personal dignity.

Personal testing is a different matter. It could give you more trouble, especially if you fail to recognize it for what it is. It may come from someone your own age or someone much older or younger. It may come from a fellow worker or it may come from someone in management. You might be wise to start out with the attitude that everything is teasing rather than testing. Then, if it doesn't last long, you have automatically solved the problem.

But if it continues over a long period of time you will know it is personal testing and it has deep-seated motives. When this happens, you have a real challenge ahead of you. For example, one of your fellow employees may refuse to accept you. He may harass you at every turn. He may not give you a chance to be a normal, productive employee. The needle will be out at every opportunity.

Ray had this kind of an experience when he was assigned to a maintenance crew with a gas and water company. The job was extremely important to him because it had taken him a long time to get it. He also knew that he was on a very strict ninety-day probation period. Because of this, Ray decided that he would go all out to keep his personal productivity high and still build good relationships with the rest of the crew.

Everything would have been great if it had not been for Art, who started out the very first day using every technique in the book to slow Ray down and get under his skin. Art constantly came up with comments like: "What are you trying to do, Ray, make us all look bad?" "Who are you kissin' up to by working so hard?" "If you slow down a little, kid, we'll get you through probation."

After three weeks of this Ray knew he was up against a personality conflict loaded with hostility. Rather than take it any longer, he invited Art to have coffee with him after work one day. It was a strained evening, but Art finally relaxed. Much of the hostility disappeared, and the next day he was off Ray's back. Ray never discovered the real cause of the conflict. The crew seemed happier, and productivity was better.

Chances are good that it will never happen to you personally, but occasionally an employee will get on the receiving end of some nonorganizational or personal testing from a supervisor. This is what happened to both Rachel and Jess.

Rachel was happy when she graduated near the top of her class in nursing school.She was even happier when she won her first job as a vocational nurse in a large home for elderly people. But Rachel, a very sincere and conscientious black, quickly discovered that she was on the receiving end of some rather vicious testing from her supervisor.

She was not surprised when she received a lot of ugly jobs her first few days. She knew it was traditional, so she pleasantly went about giving baths to some of the most difficult patients. She had many disagreeable duties, all of which were assigned to her by the supervisor, a registered nurse who had been at the home for many years.

Rachel didn't complain; she didn't want any special favors because she was black. She took everything that came her way, because she wanted to prove to herself that she could take it. But slowly she began to sense there was something more than just routine testing involved. Her supervisor seemed to dish out the ugly assignments with a strange, subtle bitterness. Not only that, but even after two new vocational nurses had joined the staff, Rachel was still doing all of the really dirty jobs.

Although she was fearful of racial prejudice from the beginning, she tried to play it cool and hope for a change. She said nothing. But soon her fellow workers, most of whom were her age and also vocational nurses, got the message. When they did, a confrontation took place that finally reached the desk of the owner. The pressure on Rachel was quickly removed, and no one was sorry a week later when the registered nurse responsible resigned.

It is sometimes impossible to know the deep-seated motives behind some of the serious testing that takes place. Often the people responsible do not know themselves. Racial prejudice is only one of many causes, as the case involving Jess will illustrate.

Jess was really pleased about his new construction job. At last he would be able to put his apprenticeship training to work and make some good money. He anticipated all of the teasing he got from the old-timers at the beginning, and he took it in stride without any big scenes. But his foreman's attitude was something else. No matter how hard he tried, Jess got the needle from his foreman at every turn. No matter how much work Jess turned out, the foreman was on his back.

Jess took it for about a week, and then, in desperation, he asked the advice of one of the older crew members. Here is what the older man said: "Look, buddy, our beloved supervisor is an uptight conservative. Your long hair, your flashy sports car, and especially your free and easy life-style all get to him. Frankly, I think he has had some trouble with his own sons and you remind him of them. At any rate, he's all wrong. What you do to get him off your back, though, is your own problem. Good luck."

Jess gave it some serious thought and decided that he would face the foreman and see what happened. It was a tough decision to make because he didn't want to lose his job. He waited until they could be alone, and then he put all his cards on the table. He said, "You've been on my back, and you know it! I think you should either tell me why or start treating me the way you treat the others." There were some tense and awkward moments, but when it was all over the foreman managed a small smile, and from then on things were noticeably better for Jess.

The above examples represent only a few of the many different cases that could be presented. Sometimes supervisors are responsible; sometimes they are not. The question is, of course, what can you do if you come up against a serious testing situation.

Here are a few pointers that may help you.

Accept the situation willingly until you have time to analyze it carefully. Take it as part of the test period and conduct yourself in such a manner as not to aggravate the situation. It may pass by itself, or someone else, without your knowledge, may come to your rescue. If time does not take care of it and you come to the point where you sincerely feel that you are being pushed too far, approach the person who is doing the needling with a "let's lay all the cards on the table" attitude. In your own words, without hostility, say something like this: "If I have done anything to upset you, please tell me. Otherwise, I feel it is time we started to respect each other."

This will not be easy for you to do. But in cases of extreme testing it is necessary for the new worker to make the tester account for his actions. There is no other answer.

Unfortunately, some individuals will push you around indefinitely if you permit it. And if you permit it, they will never respect you. Chances are that this will not happen to you, but if it does, you must stand up to the situation and solve it yourself. It is important to you and to the company that you do so.

Of course, you should go about it in the right way. Try not to have a chip on your shoulder. Do not make accusations. Try not to say anything personal about the person you are standing up to. Your goal is to open up the relationship, to find a foundation upon which you can build for the future. Your goal is to demolish the psychological barrier, not to find out who is responsible for it. You must make it easy for the other person to save face. Once the relationship is reestablished, you must follow through and do your share of rebuilding.

You will be better off if you do not go to the personnel department in such situations. You will be respected for taking care of the problem yourself. If, however, you have made every effort to clear it up over a reasonable length of time and you have had no success, you should go to your supervisor and discuss it honestly and freely. Situations of this kind should not be permitted to continue to the point where departmental morale and productivity are impaired.

It is important not to anticipate such situations. They are very rare. Such a problem may never come your way. For the most part, teasing and testing will be good-natured—maybe even enjoyable—if you have the right attitude.

PROBLEM 11
Confrontation

Jane graduated from a state college as a home-economics major. She was ambitious, talented, and determined. In practically no time she had a good position with a giant retail operation, working in a laboratory where all consumer products purchased by the buyers were tested for safety, wearability, and other standards.

Jane received many compliments on her work from her supervisor. In addition, she was able to build good relationships with all her co-workers—except Ms. Robertson. Ms. Robertson was a long-time employee of the company and very critical of Jane. She was constantly making unkind and seemingly uncalled-for remarks about Jane.

One day Jane decided to do something about it. By checking around, she discovered that two previous employees had resigned because of her. This made Jane feel that there was nothing personal about the trouble she was having. With this in mind, she waited for the right opportunity to meet Ms. Robertson alone, and this is what she said:

"Ms. Robertson, I have been here for two months and I seem to be getting along with everyone but you. I like my job. I want to keep it. If I have done something to offend you, please tell me and I'll certainly make a change. I want very much to win your respect, but I do not intend to put up with your unfair treatment of me any longer."

Did Jane do the right thing? Was she too forceful in her approach? What would you have done in her place? (For a suggested answer, see page 195).

12

Absenteeism
and
Human Relations

"Sorry I didn't show up for work yesterday, Rich. I had a little too much to drink at Harry's party so I decided to stay in the sack and sleep it off."

"Hope things weren't too hard on you last Friday, Alice. I had a case of the blahs, so I stayed home and got a few personal things taken care of."

"Knock it off, Roger, what is sick leave for if you can't steal a day for a special event now and then, or just stay home and take it easy? If you handle it right, the personnel department won't know the difference anyway."

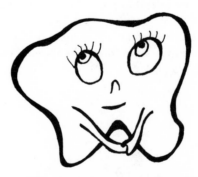

"I'm proud of my absentee record."

"Did you hear that sick crack from my supervisor, Marge? She sure gets uptight when I'm a little late now and then. You'd think that I'd committed a major crime."

"Don't breathe a word to the boss, Linda, but I'm going to make this a three-day weekend so I can go on a hiking trip. See you Tuesday."

"I've got to sneak out and take care of something personal, Art. Cover for me while I'm gone, will you?"

Absenteeism is a phenomenon that management lives with on a daily basis. So is the problem of lateness and employees leaving their work stations without authorization. Most personnel officers agree that fewer and fewer people are taking pride in their attendance or on-time records. Why?

Those close to the scene have come up with many answers. Here are four that are frequently cited: (1) young people do not commit themselves to a career or company quickly these days, so that during the exploratory stage they do not feel as much pressure to live up to the rules, (2) schools and colleges are so relaxed these days that the adjustment to the business discipline is more difficult than it was in the past, (3) many people no longer feel obligated to live up to attendance standards or rules imposed on them by organizations, and (4) people allow personal problems to spill over into their work environment more than in the past.

What is the basic policy that most business and government organizations have toward absenteeism and reporting to work late? What is acceptable and what is not? What is management's attitude toward the problem, and what action do they take with those who consistently violate their policies?

Most professional personnel managers in business and government will endorse and try to get their employees to live within the framework and spirit of the following policy:

Employees should not come to work when one of the following conditions exist: (1) when it might endanger their own health or that of their co-workers, (2) when the employee is in a psychological or emotional state that could hurt on-the-job productivity and possibly create an unsafe condition, (3) when a serious personal or family emergency exists. If none of the above conditions exists, employees should be on the job and, except in special cases, they should be there on time.

The above policy might sound harsh and autocratic, but organizations have had years of experience with the problem and they feel that unless they take a firm stand they will be misinterpreted by some and taken advantage of by others. Here are their reasons for following such a policy.

In order to make a profit and stay in business most organizations must operate under tight production and service schedules. These schedules are built around employees. An assembly line from which a few workers are absent is no longer an assembly line. When a customer wants to buy something in a retail store and there is nobody available to help him, a sale can be lost. When a customer goes to a restaurant and the waitress must do the work of two because another waitress didn't show up, the customer may never return.

Management has learned that when an employee or supervisor doesn't show up for work as scheduled, immediate and costly adjustments are necessary if production is to continue and customers are to be kept happy. Sometimes, but not always, a substitute worker can be found. Sometimes, but not always, the other employees can pitch in and fill the gap. But most of the time, the company pays at least a small price in loss of efficiency, loss of sales, or loss of customer faith. In short, the absence of an employee usually costs the company money in one way or another. If the absence is necessary, nobody complains. But if the absence is unnecessary, then management must become concerned and involved.

Chronic lateness by an employee, although not usually as serious or expensive for the company as absenteeism, is still a problem. A late employee can delay the changing of shifts. An employee who is constantly late can emotionally upset a conscientious supervisor and make her (or him) more difficult for others to work with for the rest of the day. Most serious of all is the negative influence the consistently late employee has on the productivity of others. The supervisor who takes a soft approach to such an employee stands the chance of losing the respect of other, more reliable employees.

But absenteeism, lateness, and unauthorized time away from work are not only management problems. They should also be viewed as problems and challenges to the employee himself (or herself). That is primarily what this chapter is about. How should *you* look at these problems? How will they influence *your* future?

Supervisors and workers alike who fail to build a good record in these areas will almost always pay a very high price as far as their relationships with others is concerned. Here is why.

1. A POOR ATTENDANCE RECORD WILL KEEP YOU FROM BUILDING GOOD HORIZONTAL WORKING RELATIONSHIPS WITH YOUR CO-WORKERS. THEY MAY DEEPLY RESENT HAVING TO CARRY AN EXTRA LOAD WHEN YOU ARE ABSENT. Few kinds of behavior will destroy a relationship more than being frequently absent and causing co-workers to "carry" you in your own department.

2. A POOR RECORD WILL STRAIN THE VERTICAL WORKING RELATION-SHIP WITH YOUR SUPERVISOR. IT WILL MAKE MORE WORK FOR HER (OR HIM) PERSONALLY, IT WILL CAUSE HER DEPARTMENT TO BE LESS EFFI-CIENT, AND IT WILL PUT HER ON THE SPOT WITH OTHER EMPLOYEES. Most experts agree that it is almost impossible for an employee to maintain a healthy relationship with an immediate supervisor while being guilty of chronic absenteeism.

In addition to the two basic reasons above, the four below should also receive consideration.

• Excessive absenteeism and lateness will build a credibility gap between you and management. This can seriously hurt your future, because those who cannot be depended upon are seldom promoted. It should also be pointed out that, right or wrong, some management people feel there is a moral aspect to the prob-lem. If an individual accepts employment, he or she agrees to abide by the rules, within reason. Absence without sufficient cause is interpreted by these people as moral failure.

• Records that reflect heavy absenteeism and lateness are per-manent and can be forwarded upon request to other organiza-tions. The record you are building now could help or hurt you should you decide to move elsewhere.

• If you have a good record, a request to be absent for personal and nonemergency reasons will seem more acceptable.

• In case of layoffs, cutbacks, and reassignments, those people with poor records are usually the first to be terminated or reassigned.

Most organizations want to be understanding about these problems. They realize that there are exceptions to the rules, and they are willing to listen and make adjustments. Those who consistently abuse the rules are usually counseled in a sensitive manner and given adequate warnings. Those who play it straight with their companies usually receive fair and just treatment in return. To illustrate the causes and results of absenteeism and lateness among employees and supervisors, the following six examples are cited.

Dennis was a productive worker. When he was on the job and feeling well, nobody could complain about him. He had plenty of skill, a great sense of humor, and he was always willing to pitch in and help others. His only real problem was drinking. Every other week he would really tie one on and call in sick.

About a year ago Dennis and his supervisor had a series of heart-to-heart talks about Dennis's drinking. Three months later Dennis and the personnel director discussed the problem on three different occasions. Six months ago—half a year since his first talk with the supervisor—Dennis was referred to the company physician for professional help. Last week Dennis was reluctantly given his termination notice. His record showed that he had been absent over thirty days during the previous year. The organization Dennis worked for had tried to help, but Dennis had refused to help himself.

When she first came to work, Judy showed great promise. She had all of the skills necessary to become a top-flight employee, and she was great with people. Among some of the staff in personnel she quickly became known as the "too" girl. She was too pretty, too vivacious, and too popular. She also received too many invitations to too many parties, and as a result, she was absent too frequently.

It became clear to her supervisor that Judy just didn't have the physical endurance to lead such an active social life and hold down a demanding full-time job at the same time. During the first six months of employment she was absent eleven times, each time for one day, and her excuse was always illness. After repeated counseling, Judy's supervisor finally asked personnel to transfer her to another department. Personnel made an attempt to do this, but when other supervisors checked on her absentee record, they refused to accept her. After additional, unsuccessful counseling management had to let her go.

Katherine was highly ambitious, talented, energetic, and respected by both fellow employees and management. Everybody expected her to move a long way up the executive ladder. She seemed programmed for success. But Katherine's desire for quick recognition and more money caused her to hurt her reputation inside the company. Here is the story.

Katherine took a moonlighting job with a musical group that was good enough to get four or five bookings each week. The job paid good money, but it demanded a great deal of energy. After a few months Katherine not only looked beat, but her on-the-job productivity started to drop. Soon she started to call in sick from time to time. Within six months she had seriously hurt her reputation.

Fortunately for Katherine, she had an understanding supervisor and personnel director. After some counseling, Katherine quit her moonlighting and started to build back the fine reputation she had once enjoyed. It cost her at least one promotion, but Katherine did learn one lesson: any outside activity that drains one's energy to the point where frequent absences are necessary eventually spells trouble.

Vicki was an excellent salesgirl in a fashion department. She was so good, in fact, that she was being trained as a fashion coordinator or buyer. But Vicki had one bad habit she could not shake. She simply could not organize her day to the point where she could get to work on time. Her timecard showed that she was from five to fifteen minutes late two or three times each week.

Vicki's supervisor, the personnel director, and the store manager all counseled her. Nobody wanted to lose her, but in the final analysis management had to weigh the influence of her lateness on the morale and productivity of others. When this was done, the decision to release Vicki was reluctantly made. She didn't have any trouble getting another job, but the new job didn't have the potential of the one she had lost and the new management was less tolerant of her problem.

Ralph took a job with a business organization to earn money so he could go to law school. The company had a sick-leave policy that granted ten days per year, nonaccumulative. Ralph decided that as long as he would only be around for a year, he might as well use up his sick leave as he went along. Unfortunately for Ralph, big companies are aware of this sort of thing. After being absent five times in five months, Ralph was confronted with the problem, admitted the truth, and was terminated for a basic violation of the company's sick-leave policy. Ralph didn't realize it at the time, but he paid a high price for his five days off.

A national chain organization was forced to cut back its work force because of lower sales. It was decided that they could get by with one instead of two employees in a particular department in one of their stores. One individual would be transferred to a less desirable job in another section.

A careful analysis was made to see which of the two people should be moved. Both were highly respected, and they were equal in all but two respects. One employee had three years' seniority over the other, so normally she would stay. But her absentee record was much poorer than that of the other employee. Management decided that the employee with the better attendance record deserved to keep the better job. When the employee with seniority was notified and given the reason for the decision, she admitted she had no defense.

The above cases are just a few examples of how employees can hurt their long-range careers by frequent absenteeism or chronic lateness. Here are a few tips that will help you:

1. Stay home under the following conditions: (a) when you are honestly sick and feel it would hurt your health or that of others if you reported to work, (b) when your emotional or mental condition is such that you know you could not contribute to the productivity of the department and might endanger the safety of others, and (c) when you have a family emergency and are urgently needed at home.

2. Notify the company at once of your decision to stay home. Tell them in an honest and straightforward way why you can't make it.

3. If you stay at home for more than a single day because of illness, it is wise to give personnel a daily progress report on your condition. Also estimate when you will be able to return.

4. Save your authorized sick-leave time for real emergencies.

It is a cushion that might come in handy. If you never use it, you should assume the attitude that you were lucky you didn't have to.

5. Always give yourself a little lead time when getting ready to report to work. Do not put yourself in a position where a small delay will make you late. It is better to be ten minutes early than one minute late. On those rare occasions when you are late, give management the real reason for it.

6. Take your allotted breaks, but don't be absent from your work station longer than the specified time. People who always stretch their coffee breaks are not appreciated by their co-workers or their supervisor. When emergencies do come up and you must forgo or delay a scheduled break, don't nurse a feeling that you have been cheated and that you need an extra long break to make up for it.

7. Don't be absent from your work station for long, unless you work it out in advance with your supervisor. Also, let your co-workers and/or your supervisor know where you will be when you are away. The best way to keep a supervisor from breathing down your neck is to earn your freedom by keeping him (or her) adequately informed.

8. When you have special reasons for being absent from work, such as family weddings, funerals, or court appearances, work it out as far in advance as possible with your supervisor and the personnel department.

A good record shows management your interest in your job, the company, and its goals. It shows them that you are a motivated rather than reluctant worker. It shows them that you have a positive attitude about your career.

Build a good attendance record, and you'll build a good reputation with management. Maintain a good on-time record, and you'll get along better with your supervisor. Take pride in being a dependable worker and you'll build much better relationships with your fellow workers. Put it all together and you'll be much happier with yourself and with your career.

PROBLEM 12
Habits

It didn't come as a surprise to Gary's friends when they heard he was in trouble with his company because of absenteeism and chronic lateness. It was the same pattern he had followed on campus—always missing classes and always showing up late. Of course, it was a little different on campus, because he could turn on his charm and manipulate teachers. With his immediate supervisor, personnel people, and other company managers, however, it was another matter.

Gary was called on the carpet for the third time three months after he started the management training program. Everybody was nice in his approach to the problem, but it was finally made clear that Gary should either start changing his habits or consider working elsewhere. The strange thing about it all was that Gary really wanted to be successful. It was a good job. It was a fine company.

Why had he permitted himself to build such a poor record? Here are three reasons: (1) he had underestimated how difficult it would be to change the habits he had developed in school, (2) he couldn't bluff as easily in the business world, and (3) he failed to understand that by being late or absent he was hurting his relationships with others because it put an extra burden on their shoulders.

At any rate, Gary admitted that he had started off on the wrong foot. He did have a poor record as far as absenteeism and lateness were concerned. He did have a reputation for being undependable. Now he had a very difficult decision to make. Should he stick with his company, try to change his habits, and work hard to live down the poor record? Or should he resign and start over with a new company?

What would you advise Gary to do? (For a suggested answer see page 196.)

13

Three Common Human Relations Mistakes

In business operations today many new, ambitious employees make human-relations mistakes that damage their personal progress. It is the purpose of this chapter to single out and fully explain the implications of three of the most common mistakes.

1. Failure to listen.
2. Underestimating others.
3. Failure to report or admit mistakes to management.

Failure to Listen

Many excellent books and articles have been written about the art of listening. Some of these have been researched and written

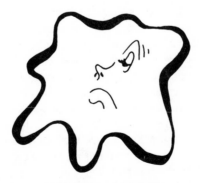

"Me? Make a mistake?"

by specialists. Your public library will help you find worthwhile material on the subject. Our discussion of it will be brief and to the point.

Many people need to *learn how to listen*. They must learn how to *concentrate*.

Hearing is a selective process. You can, with concentration, hear what you want to hear. Your problem, then, is to learn to listen to what is important and push other sounds to the outer edge of your hearing. There are so many sounds around you that you may not be picking up the ones that are vital to your happiness and success.

On the job, hearing is a matter of practical communication. When a supervisor or fellow worker wishes to transmit an idea, a warning, or a change in procedure to you, he (or she) usually does it verbally. There may not be time for written communication. Conditions may not be ideal. There may be other sounds he cannot eliminate. It may be the end of the day, and you may be tired. His words may mean one thing to him and another to you. Good, clear, accurate communication is never easy.

Let us assume, however, that the person initiating the message does the best job possible. Does this ensure that you will receive the message? Of course not! You are the receiver, and if your mind is focused elsewhere when the message is transmitted, *you may hear the sounds but fail to get the message*.

It is evident that communication is a complicated process. It is not easy to be a good sender or a good receiver. Let's take a closer look at the problem.

Advertising executives and specialists have recognized for years how difficult it is to get the verbal message home. This difficulty is most apparent in television commercials. There, the name of the product is often repeated six times in thirty seconds. If you are really listening, you might feel that such repetition is an insult to your ability to receive. You would be justified in this reaction. But the advertising people do not assume that you are a good listener. They assume that you are a *typical* (that is, poor) listener. Consequently, in order for the product name to make an impression, they pound it home through repetition.

Your supervisor is not an advertising expert, nor does she (or he) have the time to pound her message home. She feels she should be able to say it once and you should receive it. She must assume you are a good listener.

You often hear a mother say that she must shout to get the message across to her young son. As sender, she is in a frustrating position. "He just doesn't listen to me anymore," she says. And the son may have the same complaint: "There's no use talking to my mother. She just doesn't listen, so how can she understand me?" Perhaps both mother and son have forgotten how to listen.

This can happen to people with the best of intentions. Sometimes it is very difficult just to sit back and listen. There are three basic reasons why this is true. First, we are often so busy with our own thoughts and desires, related or nonrelated, that we are 90 percent sender and only 10 percent receiver. When this happens, the communication system breaks down. Second, some individuals are self-centered. Instead of hearing what is being said, they are merely waiting for the speaker to finish so that they can then talk. Getting their thoughts organized keeps them from being good listeners. Third, some people allow themselves to analyze motives or personality traits of the person speaking and, again, fail to hear what is said.

In business and industry, the ability of the employee to listen is often a matter of dollars and cents. A draftsman who doesn't hear an architect tell him to make a certain change in a blueprint can cause the loss of thousands of dollars when a bid is accepted on specifications that are not correct. A salesman who fails to hear a message from a client, and as a result does not comply with an important delivery date, can lose not only the sale but also a valuable customer.

Communications problems can also cost money inside factories. For example, Daniel's failure to receive and retain the right message from his shop foreman cost his company a considerable amount of money. Here is the story.

On his way to his regular morning coffee break and somewhat preoccupied with his own thoughts, Dan was stopped by his foreman and told to change the tolerance on a machine part he would be turning out for the rest of the day. After his coffee break, Dan returned to his machine, made an adjustment, and worked hard the rest of the day to complete all of the parts. The following day he was called on the carpet for producing parts that were too small. What had happened? Dan had been told to *increase* the size of the part, but he had *decreased* it instead. His failure to receive —and retain—the right message was a serious mistake, and it cost his company money in terms of both time and materials.

You can think of many other examples. It can even be said that when safety precautions are the subject of the message, the ability to listen can be a matter of life or death.

Let's look at your ability to listen from the viewpoint of your supervisor who is, after all, the primary sender of important messages to you. Here are four questions you can ask yourself to determine whether you are a good listener:

1. Does your supervisor have to fight to get your attention?

2. Do you find yourself thinking about something else the moment he starts talking?

3. Does he voluntarily repeat the message? Or do you find you must go back and ask him to repeat it?

4. Do you sometimes feel confused about instructions given to you when you start to do the job requested?

If you can say no to these questions, you may be a good listener. If not, you should concentrate on improving. The following tips should help you.

1. Always look at the person who is sending the message; this will help you to concentrate and close out unimportant noises.

2. If your supervisor has trouble sending clear signals, you must make the extra effort to listen more carefully. Although it is primarily his responsibility to be a good sender, it is still to your advantage to receive the message if at all possible.

3. So that you will remember the message, jot it down in your notebook. Repeat it in your own mind a few times. Put any change ordered in the message into practice as soon as possible. When appropriate, repeat the message to your supervisor.

4. Refrain from coming up with an excuse when you receive criticism. You will improve more if you listen to what you are doing wrong rather than quickly coming to your own defense.

5. Think, reply briefly if necessary, and then continue to listen so that you receive the complete concept.

6. Always ask questions *right away* if you don't understand something. If you don't do this you may not fully get the message that follows.

7. If you find yourself in conversation with someone who is overtalking do not hesitate to interrupt after a polite period of time. If you do not do this you may become so irritated you may not listen anyway.

Being a good listener is not easy. It will take a conscientious effort on your part. But one of the finest compliments you will ever receive will be something like this: "One thing I really like about him is that if you tell him something once you know he's got it. You never have to tell him twice."

Being a good listener will pay handsome dividends!

Underestimating Others

The second of the three big mistakes, according to personnel people, is that of underestimating others, particularly those in management postitions. One of the mistakes you can make most easily is to underestimate the contribution of another person to the productivity of your organization.

As a nonsupervisor new to the organization, you cannot see the overall picture. You have no way of knowing the multiple responsibilities faced by other people. A management or non-management person may not appear to be doing very much from your limited perspective. You might wrongly assume that he or she is coasting. This could be a big mistake.

Here is a simple case to emphasize the point.

Henry accepted a job with a major metropolitan department store. After thirty days of training he was temporarily assigned to the basement operation. His supervisor was Ms. Smith, the manager of inexpensive women's apparel.

Henry soon discovered that he was part of a rather hectic operation. Merchandise moved in and out of the department quickly. Racks and counters were messy and disorganized. Ms. Smith was not an impressive person to Henry. Her desk was disorderly. She seemed to move in many directions at the same time. She seemed to spend more time than necessary talking to the employees.

Henry decided that he had drawn an unfortunate first assignment. He wished he could move to the upper floors where there was more prestige and where the managers seemed to be better organized.

It was his good luck, however, to meet a young buyer at lunch one day. From this woman he learned that Ms. Smith had the most profitable department in the store and an outstanding reputation with all top management people. Ms. Smith had trained more of the store's executives than any other person. It was then obvious that Henry had received one of the best assignments and had seriously underestimated Ms. Smith.

The new employee in this case learned a big lesson without getting hurt. He quickly changed his attitude toward his supervisor before the relationship was seriously damaged. He was fortunate.

The danger is great when you fail to build a good relationship with a supervisor or a fellow employee because you underestimate her (or him).

You, as a new employee, are in the poorest position to estimate the power, influence, and contribution that others are making to the organization, *especially when these people are already in management positions.* You will be smart to avoid prejudging others. Different people make different contributions to the growth and profit of an organization. Top management can usually see this, but you usually cannot.

If the temptation is too great and you must at times question the effectiveness of others, keep your impressions to yourself. You can easily trap yourself by being a Monday morning quarterback. Underestimating the value of others can cost you a great deal in personal progress.

Failure to Report or Admit Mistakes to Management

The third common human-relations mistake is failure to admit or report to management personal errors in judgment or violations of company procedures, rules, and regulations.

Everyone makes minor slips and blunders from time to time. Even a good employee is not perfect. Precise and methodical people sometimes make mistakes in calculations. Logical thinkers who pride themselves on their scientific approach to decision making will sometimes make an error in judgment. A conscientious person who is very loyal to his organization will, on occasion, violate a company rule or regulation before he knows it.

These things happen to the best of people, and unless you are a most unusual person they will happen to you. These little mistakes will not damage your career if you admit them openly. They can, however, cause considerable damage if you try to cover them up and in so doing compound the original mistake. To illustrate, let us take the incident of the dented fender.

Ken had started his career with a large banking organization six months before. One of his numerous responsibilities in his first assignment was to deliver important documents to various branch operations in the banking system. To do this, he would check out a company car from the transportation department.

On one such assignment, Ken dented the fender of a company car while backing out of a crowded parking lot. He knew that he should report the damage to the dispatcher, but the dent was so insignificant that he thought it would go unnoticed. Why make a federal case out of a little scratch? Why spoil a clean record with the company over something so unimportant?

Two days later Ken was called into the private office of his department manager. It was an embarrassing twenty minutes. He had to admit that he was responsible for the damage and that he had broken a company rule by not reporting it. The incident was then closed.

The slight damage to the company car was a human error anyone could make. The *big* mistake Ken made was in not reporting it. Looking back on the incident, he admitted that the damage to the car was far less than the damage to his relationships with others.

Most little mistakes, and sometimes many big mistakes, are accepted and forgotten when they are openly and quickly reported. But to throw up a smoke screen to cover them up is to ask for unnecessary trouble. The second mistake may be more damaging than the first.

PROBLEM 13
Listening

Fay was a recent graduate of a metropolitan art institute that had an outstanding reputation. The instructors at the institute were so pleased with her work that they went out on a limb to help her get her first job with a large advertising agency.

After a few weeks on the job it became obvious to everyone that Fay had unusual talent. It also became obvious that she was a great talker and a lousy listener. She would bubble over in communicating her own ideas, but the moment someone else started to talk, her attention would drift. One person interpreted this behavior as a form of discourtesy and tried to stay clear of Fay.

Fay's job consisted primarily of doing preliminary sketches and renderings of assorted products, forms, and symbols. These were communicated to her verbally by her supervisor, a talented artist himself. Often he would take only a few minutes to explain what he wanted and then leave Fay to work away for the rest of the day.

Although Fay's finished artwork was very exciting, her supervisor soon became impatient with her inability to produce work even remotely related to the ideas he had given her verbally. Most of what she turned in had to be thrown away. After giving it some serious thought, Fay's boss came to the conclusion that she got so emotionally charged when discussing various art concepts that she just didn't hear what other people, including himself, were saying. Finally he called her into his office and told her she would either have to learn to listen or he would have to recommend her release.

Was Fay's boss justified in his impatience and the action he finally took? What suggestions would you make to her in order to solve the problem and save her job? (For a suggested answer, see page 197.)

14

Beware of
the Rumor Mill

Webster's New World Dictionary gives us this definition of the word *rumor*: "General talk not based on definite knowledge; mere gossip; hearsay; an unconfirmed report, story, or statement in general circulation."

Unauthenticated reports, or rumors, seem to originate and circulate within every group of people, expecially when members of such a group have common interests and competitive goals. Rumors are common in small communities, social and service groups, schools, churches, and, of course, business organizations.

Rumors are based on people's need to share their anxieties with others. Some rumors get started because of faulty communication or unintentional misinterpretation of the original message. Others are in the form of malicious gossip designed to hurt another person.

Two popular expressions have become associated with the circulation of rumors. One is *rumor mill*. This familiar expression

"Another rumor on its way."

implies that rumors, like grain being processed in a mill, are turned out regularly in large numbers, altered, and circulated within the confines of a certain group or organization.

The second popular expression is *grapevine*, which means an unofficial, confidential, person-to-person chain of verbal communication. The grapevine can best be viewed as an underground network that operates within an organization. The rumor mill may get the message started but the grapevine keeps it moving. The grapevine has the reputation of operating without official sanction, and usually the information transmitted has an aura of secrecy.

Not all information that gets into the rumor mill and travels along the grapevine is false. It can be the truth. But the person who introduces the information must have the facts right and those facts must be transmitted without misinterpretation. These conditions are, of course, seldom present. Even when the original information is accurate, facts can become distorted as they move along the grapevine.

The important thing to realize is that information processed through the rumor mill and passed along the grapevine is *not* reliable.

It may not be based upon the facts. It may be slanted to serve the interests of a second, third, or fourth party. It may even be malicious.

For these reasons the rumor mill should be viewed with considerable caution, and information coming through the grapevine should be discounted. You cannot depend on it.

Since rumors occur in all organizations, it is only natural to find them in business and industrial concerns, and it follows that there may be a rumor mill in your organization. If there is, stand forewarned.

What is management's position in this matter? This book, of course, cannot speak for your particular management. However, this much can be said: the term *rumor mill* is not new to those in leadership positions and management usually knows when a grapevine exists.

This does not mean that the people responsible for management condone the grapevine, but they know when it is in operation. We know this because they occasionally step in and squelch a false rumor before damage is done to either an individual or the company.

The new worker should realize that keeping employees fully informed on company matters is a huge task. Conferences, bulletins, company periodicals, and other media are often not effective. But even if official forms of communication were fully adequate, it is doubtful that rumors would be eliminated. Management knows this. So if you are on the receiving end of rumors in your job and you sense the existence of rumor mill, this does not mean that management is not concerned. It is!

Management is aware that unfounded rumors can cause unnecessary anxiety among employees and that such anxiety hurts the morale of the organization. They know that efficiency drops when personnel are unsettled by information that is false or half-true. They know that rumors can sometimes be malicious, and that innocent employees can be hurt. They will do what they can to prevent this.

In order to be successful, however, they need the help and support of every employee.

What might you do to help management? And more important, what might you do to help yourself? Here are six suggestions.

1. The first thing is to admit that there *is* such a phenomenon as a rumor mill in your organization. If you are blind to this situation you may introduce and transmit harmful rumors to others without knowing it.

2. All information received through the grapevine, especially if it has implications of intrigue, should be viewed with skepticism, and you should not permit this information to disturb you personally. If it is true, you will have time to adjust to it after you receive it from official sources. Be patient until you get the facts. Partial information is dangerous. Give management time to give you all the facts. Do not take any action or make decisions until you *know*.

3. Do not be guilty yourself of introducing rumors into the grapevine. You may, by accident, overhear something of a confidential nature and pass it on to someone as the truth, only to discover at a later date that you only heard part of the story. Or you may see something a little unusual and draw the wrong conclusion, as in the following case.

Rebecca noticed her supervisor, a young married man, taking her co-worker Florence, who was divorced, home two nights in succession. She decided there was something going on between them and introduced the matter into the local grapevine. As so often happens, the rumor got out of hand. A number of people, including Rebecca herself, got hurt. The supervisor was transferred and his replacement was harsh and demanding. What was the truth? Florence had put her car in the repair shop for two days, and the supervisor had volunteered to take her home so that she would not have to walk the dark streets alone. There was nothing more involved.

4. Refuse to pass on unsubstantiated information you receive secondhand. If you do this, you may break the circuit in the grapevine and perhaps keep others from becoming disturbed unnecessarily. Sometimes, during coffee-break talk for instance, it may be possible to steer conversation away from rumors and into harmless tracks such as sports or TV shows.

5. If you must complain about company matters or company people, do so in the proper manner to your immediate supervisor, or blow off steam at home or with a trusted person—but not with your fellow workers. This will eliminate the possibility of having your personal gripes misinterpreted and introduced into the rumor mill. It will also keep anyone from using your complaints to hurt your relationships with your superiors.

6. Try not to let a nonpersonal rumor that might involve your future with the company upset you until you get the facts. If you do, there might be a noticeable drop in your personal productivity that will needlessly hurt your future. Make every effort to ignore the rumor until you receive official information. If you find you cannot do this, consult your supervisor or someone else in management for the facts before you draw unwarranted conclusions. Many employees have injured their future by premature action based upon a false rumor. Don't fall into this trap.

We could fill pages discussing the various kinds of rumors that travel along the grapevine. We could give many examples. It will serve our purpose best, however, to place them all into the following two broad classifications.

Many on-the-job rumors involve people's personal lives and are not related to job situations. Some of these fall into the back-fence category. Some are little more than coffee-break gossip. They are important in the world of work *only* when they influence productivity. Although there is considerable intrigue to such rumors, the new employee would be wise to keep working relationships strictly *working relationships* and stay a safe distance from such rumors.

Rumors of the second kind concern the *organization*. They pertain to things that may or may not happen to the company itself. Although they influence employees, they are not personal. For example, there have been rumors about layoffs with no foundation in fact, rumors that departments were to be eliminated when in fact they were to be enlarged, rumors of resignations when in face none were ever contemplated, and rumors of terminations that turned out to be transfers.

Organizational rumors have great influence on the productivity of employees and the general progress of the company. Management, by keeping the official channels of communication open, tries to eliminate them. Rumors continue to exist in most companies, however. Unless the employee develops a way to insulate himself (or herself) against them, he can become constantly insecure about his job and his future. His personal productivity will go up and down based upon the latest rumor. And all for nothing!

Let's now look closely at one aspect of the problem from a positive point of view. Have you ever heard the expression *confidence triangle*? A confidence triangle is the way a confidential comment can be transmitted to a third party. The diagram below will help explain the idea.

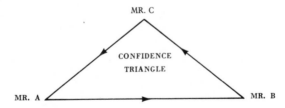

We will assume you are Mr. A. You have a strong, healthy relationship with Mr. B. Occasionally you talk things over with him in confidence. One day at lunch you mention that Mr. C has been of great help to you in completing a certain project, and that you have considerable respect for his ability and perception.

You do not realize, when you say this, that Mr. C has a strong, healthy relationship with Mr. B and that your comments will be transmitted to him. Of course, this will not hurt your relationship with Mr. C. In fact it will improve it, because these favorable comments have been made in confidence and transmitted by a person Mr. C respects.

So far, the confidence triangle has worked in a positive manner. *But what if your comments had been negative?* Instead of improving your relationships with Mr. B and Mr. C, they would have been damaged. The confidence triangle works both ways. The truth is, then, that you can strengthen or weaken relationships with some people *through others*. When you say something positive about a third person to an individual with whom you have a good rapport, relationships can improve. When you say something negative, the opposite can happen.

Nobody likes to accept advice. Even when advice comes at the right time from the right person in the right way, it is difficult to accept. Yet, sometimes accepting advice is the smart thing to do.

Let us assume that at this very moment the conditions are ideal and you are willing to accept advice. What might be the best human-relations advice you could receive? In all probability it would be this:

If you can't say something good about a person, don't say anything at all.

Like most advice that comes in such simple terms, this precept is far easier to put into print than to put into practice. Yet the degree to which you observe this simple rule on your new job will have considerable influence on your success.

Understanding the nature of rumors, the power of the rumor mill, the scope of the grapevine, and the impact of the confidence triangle should teach you to be *most* careful about what you say to others.

It has been said that many human-relations problems are self-created problems. There is truth in this statement.

PROBLEM 14
Dilemma

Sylvia was young, serious-minded, well educated, and capable. More than anything else she wanted a management role with her company.

Sylvia worked hard for three years. She did an excellent job in human relations. Her personal productivity was never questioned. Ms. Smith, her supervisor, encouraged her to prepare to take over her job. She helped Sylvia a great deal in this respect, but, of course, she could make no promises.

About this time, Sylvia spent the evening with Helen, an intimate friend of hers. At one point Helen told Sylvia she had heard that a Mr. Young, an employee from another department, was being trained to take Ms. Smith's place as department head.

Although she said nothing and did not show it on the outside, Sylvia was very disturbed by the news. It was hard to believe that management could make such a decision so far in advance. She fretted about it constantly and could not keep her mind on her work. As a result, she made more and more mistakes, and certain important reports were turned in late. Over the next six months the excellent relationship she had with her supervisor slowly deteriorated.

Then, just as Helen had said, Ms. Smith was promoted and Mr. Young was made department head in an official announcement from top management. Sylvia was deeply hurt and disappointed.

What mistakes did Sylvia make that might have contributed to her ultimate disappointment? (For a suggested answer, see page 198.)

15

Two Routes
to the
Top

There are two basic ways in which employees can build their careers and reach upper management levels. One is to join and stay with the same large organization. The other is to move from one to another when you can improve your role. The first approach we will call "PFW"; the second, "zigzag."

If you go about it in the right way, you can build a rich and rewarding career within the framework of a single organization instead of moving from one company to another. The practice that makes this possibility exciting is called *promotion from within*, or PFW.

"I'll show 'em!"

There is nothing new about PFW. It has always been the custom to move those who demonstrate they are capable and responsible into higher positions when vacancies occur. If the right people are available, *management wants to promote from within the company's own ranks.* This policy encourages loyalty, provides motivation, and has many other advantages. It should be remembered, however, that even companies that have such a policy must make a few exceptions. Management may find it necessary to bring a few outsiders, such as lawyers, architects, research specialists, and tax experts, into key staff positions.

In order to understand the implications of the PFW idea in the modern corporation, one first needs to understand the complexity of the organizational structure. Every company has grown to maturity in a different way. Every company has a history all its own. Every company has its own interpretation of PFW.

Because of this, generalizations are very dangerous. The reader must interpret the following pages in the light of policies and practices of his or her own company. One cannot presume to speak for all managements.

It is important, however, to give the new worker a perspective on his or her career possibilities. The triangle shown will get us started.

TOP MANAGEMENT

MIDDLE MANAGEMENT

JUNIOR MANAGEMENT

SUPERVISORY POSITIONS

PERSONNEL

This diagram could represent a business, industrial, or governmental organization. Size is not important. It could be a company with 200,000 employees or one with 200. Management—those people who are responsible for the leadership and direction of the company—is of course at the apex of the triangle. Some organizations divide management into four classifications: top management, middle management, junior management, and supervisory positions.

Top management executives with giant concerns are usually the president and vice-presidents. Middle-management people are usually division heads and branch and plant managers. Junior management includes middle-management assistants, those whose positions fall just beneath the middle-management classification. Next in line come the many supervisors.

Below the management level are many kinds of personnel, depending on the type of organization. In a manufacturing business we find different levels of technical people: engineers, technicians, skilled craftsmen, semiskilled workers, and helpers. In other kinds of organizations there are different patterns and different backgrounds.

Supervisory positions, as illustrated above, can outnumber higher management positions. There is usually a supervisory position for every twelve employees in an organization; in some companies the ratio is lower. The supervisory position is extremely important to the new worker, for in most cases this is the first position leading to upper management.

Now that we have seen the top of the triangle, let us look at the bottom. All organizations employ the majority of new workers at lower-level entry positions. This is where you, the new employee, will no doubt start. Of course, in most companies, entry levels depend on experience and education. With rare exceptions, however, all are close to the bottom. The following diagram will illustrate four possible entry levels for those leaving school with little or no experience.

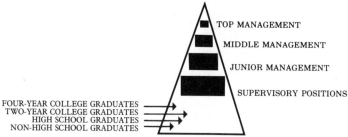

Not all companies have four entry levels. Some have only two or three. The important thing is that they are all relatively close together. Regardless of the amount of education, almost everyone starts near the bottom.

The level of the entry position, important as it may be, is not as important as the fact that all employees have an opportunity to *grow*. Each employee, regardless of where he or she starts, can and should move upward in the organization. No one is stuck forever with his entry position. This is the meaning of PFW.

This, of course, is all hypothetical. Does it always happen that way? Not necessarily. There are no guarantees.

PFW does not give the highly educated person a sure ticket to move ahead faster. He or she *should* move ahead faster. Management *expects* him to move ahead faster. He is often given special training to help him move ahead faster. But there is no guarantee. For example, in recent years affirmative action programs have permitted certain minority people to move ahead fast in order to achieve a more balanced mix of ethnic groups and women at higher management levels. This, of course, has in turn slowed down the upward movement of other lower-level employees.

The differences in people's educational backgrounds may cause human-relations problems. You know the story. The college graduate may feel she (or he) is not given opportunity fast enough. The noncollege person feels that graduates are given opportunity too fast. Management needs both and recognizes the need to give both growth opportunities. But one thing should be made clear:

The college graduate does not arrive at the top only because of the degree itself. If she arrives at all, it is because she had a greater potential and *used* it.

By the same token, the new worker is not necessarily restricted just because he (or she) does not have a degree. He can still arrive at the top and sometimes does. This may not be as universally true today as it was years ago, but it is still true. Remember, there are different ways and different routes by which a person can reach the top. And what is to keep the ambitious noncollege person from continuing his or her education at night? He may or may not eventually receive a degree, but his work in that direction will improve his potential.

A college degree is often more important to the person who doesn't have it than it is to the person who does. The danger to the noncollege person is when he permits the degree to become a psychological block. A person doesn't stop growing and learning just because he has less formal education than others. In most organizations opportunities lie in so many directions that the noncollege employee can find excellent opportunities open to him.

There is also a real danger for the college person. He may expect his college degree to open doors for him automatically. He may want too much too fast. He may expect too much status from his job at the start. In most instances he must add to his college training the practical experience the noncollege person already has before he can expect to move upward. It takes time and excellent human-relations skills to capitalize on a college education.

There are both advantages and disadvantages in building a lifetime career within the framework of an organization with a firm PFW policy. Here are three primary advantages.

1. Young people who join PFW companies compete *only* with those inside the company for better positions. They do not have to worry about outsiders who might be hired to fill positions they aspire to. Everyone starts near the bottom, and theoretically everyone has a chance to compete, despite differences in education and experience. When someone at the top retires, a chain reaction can open up many positions all the way down the organizational ladder.

2. Organizations with PFW policies are forced to provide good training for their employees so that they are ready to assume more responsibility when opportunities arise. This usually means that more on-the-job time is spent on training of all kinds. It also usually means that such companies will encourage their employees to continue their formal education and will often pay the bills. Because of this, employees are less likely to be ignored or lost in the shuffle.

3. Almost everyone is provided a high degree of job security and a growth pattern that, as far as possible, fits his individual needs. Everyone is encouraged to reach his or her own potential. Fewer people find themselves at a permanent dead end early in their careers. More individual counseling and consideration usually takes place.

Just as there are many advantages, there are also disadvantages to working for a company that has a firm PFW policy. Here are three.

1. Many highly ambitious people who work for PFW companies claim that promotions come too slowly. People are trained too far ahead of time. There is too much waiting. These are usually the same people who claim that the best way to the top is to

move from company to company instead of sticking it out with one organization.

2. The human-relations role is more critical because management and nonmanagement people seldom leave the organization and seldom forget anything. In short, a person who makes a serious human-relations mistake inside a PFW company must live with it longer, because the people affected will be around to remember.

3. More conformity may be necessary. PFW organizations seem to build a company identity that pulls people together but at the same time leaves less room for individual freedom. For some people this could be a serious disadvantage.

The zigzag is another approach to the whole matter of career planning and upward movement. It is illustrated below. It is logical to build a case that certain highly aggressive and nonconforming individuals should not attempt to stay inside a strong PFW company. They are simply not geared for the long, slow climb to the top. Rather, they should seek out companies that do not have a firm PFW policy and take the zigzag route to the top by moving from company to company whenever they can improve their position.

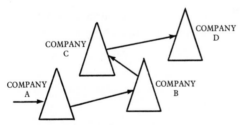

The difference between being aggressive and being assertive is important to understand in this situation. Aggressive means full of enterprise and initiative, bold and active, but not militant. Assertive means persistently positive and confident. Obviously both aggressive and assertive people are needed in all organizations, but the *highly* aggressive person might overfrustrate himself (or herself) by staying inside a strong PFW organization.

There are many good and bad factors about the zigzag route. Here are some of the advantages.

1. For those who are sufficiently aggressive and make the effort to seek out profitable transfers, the route to the top can be faster.

2. Sometimes an individual can achieve a wider and more valuable learning background by moving from one company to another. In other words, he (or she) can discover the best in each company and take it with him on to the next.

3. It is easier to leave any serious human-relations mistakes behind. This might include any unresolved human conflicts or personality differences.

Just as there are advantages, there are also disadvantages to the zigzag route.

1. Most people agree that it takes more energy to build an industry-wide reputation to insure that profitable transfers come your way. There is a degree of risk involved. You could discover after getting inside an organization and making a full evaluation that the move was a mistake.

2. Making transfers often means uprooting the entire family, and making profound personal and social—as well as professional —changes in your life.

3. Certain benefits, like profit-sharing, cannot always be transferred from one company to another without a loss or adjustment.

As you look ahead—as you plan your career—take the following factors into consideration. Although they can be important in other organizations, *they are doubly important inside a PFW company.*

• A company interested in its future must employ young people more on the basis of what they can learn in the future than on what they have learned in the past. It is the capacity to grow that is important.

• The longer you stay with a given company the more opportunities open up for you providing you continue to learn and maintain good human relationships.

• Take the broad learning approach during your early years. Move horizontally into every possible department, whether the move gives you an increase in pay or not. All experience has value as far as preparing you for positions further up the management ladder.

• Discover and study the various lines of progression in your company. Attempt to move up through the channel that best suits your ability.

• Within bounds, do not fear being aggressive. Submit ideas that have been well researched. Communicate upwards.

• When a position becomes vacant, let management know in the right way that you are interested. Do not assume that they know. It doesn't hurt your relationships with others to ask.

PROBLEM 15
Preference

Angelo was a college dropout who had nevertheless received excellent training in business management while he was enrolled. He was now twenty-two and married. Angelo was considered by his close friends to be a strong leader, highly ambitious, independent, frequently impatient, and easily frustrated.

Angelo was interviewed the same week by company A and company B. After more than two weeks of investigation both companies offered him good jobs. Company A was a dynamic, risk-taking corporation that made little effort to develop its own people. In fact, it took great delight in hiring top people away from competitive companies. They were interested in Angelo primarily because of his leadership ability and the fact that he would become immediately productive as an employee.

Company B, on the other hand, was a slow, steady company that offered a great deal of security to employees. They had a very firm PFW policy. They liked Angelo primarily because of his long-range potential and his apparent human-relations sensitivity.

Although the starting salary with company A was substantially higher, the training program with company B was superior. *All other significant factors were similar*. Which company do you think Angelo should have gone with? What factors should he have considered in making his decision? (For a suggested answer, see page 198.)

16

Plateau
Periods

The virtue of patience takes on a new dimension when a person is ambitious and anxious to build a successful career within an organization but suddenly runs into a plateau. A *plateau* is defined as a long waiting period where the role and the responsibility of the employee remains static. Small automatic or cost-of-living pay increases may occur but significant jumps do not. Sometimes plateau periods can last for years.

Why are they so difficult to live through?

In the first place, business and industry seem to intensify the problem because they seek out and hire highly ambitious people. They want and need dynamic men and women. They want and need people with energy. They want and need the competitive spirit in new employees.

But after employment it is often necessary to turn around and ask these same people to be patient.

"It takes time in any organization, Laura. Your day will come. Just sit tight and *wait*. You'll see."

"Things sure move slow around here."

"You are doing great, Joe. Just *wait* for the right opportunity and you'll be off and running."

"Continue to prepare, Henry. Learn all you can in your present job. You are in a plateau period but you will get your chance. Just *wait* and see."

The "patience suit" that management people used to suggest people wear during plateau periods becomes too tight, too confining, too uncomfortable. It is not always the fault of the organization or the individual. The problem is rooted deeply in our modern culture.

Patience isn't something one learns in school or college. Indeed, the pattern of almost automatic promotions in school is the direct opposite of what is found in the world of work. Through our school systems, people become accustomed to promotions according to age. They start at the first grade and move up to the twelfth and beyond like clockwork—each year a step up, until regular promotions are expected without waiting. Small wonder that some people begin to think that life is one progressive step after another whether the step has been truly *earned* or not.

Our society contributes in other ways to this "make it in a hurry" attitude. Both economic and social upward mobility has been the pattern for most Americans in the past few decades. As a result, most young people whose parents have "made it" have been raised in an affluent environment. Why should they wait around for thirty years to get to the same point? Why should they wait until they're ready to retire to make it, when they might do it by the time they're thirty?

Yet when they get their first job, many young people must start at the bottom with a relatively low income, inflationary prices, and no fixed promotion schedule to depend upon. Small wonder that many become impatient and seek shortcuts to better positions and higher incomes.

There are many reasons for plateau periods. The following quotations from three ambitious individuals are examples.

"I work for a fine company but we have been undergoing an unavoidable retrenchment program for over three years. There has been a freeze on new hires and promotions. I think things will open up soon but, believe me, it has not been easy to readjust my personal goals and keep my attitude from showing."

"In our organization everyone must sweat out a long plateau between junior- and middle-management roles. I have had three front-line supervisory roles over the past few years, each with more responsibility. My next jump will be into middle management. But there are many people waiting ahead of me. If I could make a move to a competing company I might save myself a few years of waiting."

"I was all set to move into a role I had spent three years preparing for when my organization went through a consolidation period and transferred the position I wanted to another city. Not wanting to move there, I had to readjust my goals into another area. So here I am, in another plateau period."

Even when things are normal inside business organizations, promotions are not automatic. In fact, management is not always aware of the growth, potential, and patience of their employees. So how is one to cope?

First, the ambitious employee should learn as much as possible about plateau periods so that he or she can wear a "patience suit" gracefully. Second, he should study ways in which such periods can be shortened.

Business and industrial leaders believe in *promotion by merit.*

They know that the opportunity to succeed in open competition with others provides the vitality their organizations must have. Seniority, experience, and age are not always enough to win a given promotion. The new worker can to some degree set his (or her) own pattern of promotion, provided that he demonstrates capability.

Promotion by merit is quite different from automatic promotion. When the eager, resourceful employee reaches a plateau—while hoping instead for a promotion—the patience suit becomes more and more uncomfortable. The opportunities to move up still exist, of course, but they sometimes come slowly and only after long periods of waiting.

These periods of waiting are critical for the career employee.

They can destroy confidence.

They can create problems.

They can cause needless turnover.

But far more important than all other factors is the attitude and productivity of the employee during such periods of waiting.

When the career employee going through a plateau period permits his (or her) attitude and productivity to drop substantially, then he defeats himself. At the very point in his career when he should be working up to his potential, he often slips the most. When this happens, the plateau is often extended by management and others are given the promotional opportunities that exist.

It is not an easy thing to ask an aggressive person to wear a patience suit, but management often has no alternative. Opportunities can and do open up in organizations overnight, but it is almost impossible to produce a steady flow of opportunities to fit the time schedules of individuals.

Management cannot eliminate all of the pressure points that the new employee often faces. Salary schedules cannot be quickly adjusted to the needs of each individual. Unexpected family expenses cannot always be taken care of by company insurance programs.

Management people can, however, understand the frustration that comes when a promising career gets temporarily bogged down. They know because they have usually been there themselves. They know it is a difficult period. They know it is a time when some people begin to question seriously their goals. They know it is a time when personal values are challenged. They know it is a time when some start to think about returning to college for more formal education.

One large financial organization has actually gone so far as to chart out a leveling-off or "wait-out" period. They have named it the *big plateau*. New employees in this company usually make steady progress over the first few years, but the big jump from their first supervisory position to middle management often requires a long period of waiting. It may be one, two, three, or more years, because at this level management positions open up very slowly. The problem has become so critical that, once these employees reach the big plateau, the company attempts to provide more counseling to help them over the hump.

Carving out a career inside a large company requires some waiting, even when the patience suit becomes most uncomfortable. The very word *career* implies steady progress, not speedy progress.

Being ambitious and capable has never been easy in our society. When a person is in her (or his) twenties, a year may seem more like five years. And yet many employees are past thirty before they have an opportunity to fully demonstrate their true ability.

True, a few people do find success early. The entertainment field, professional sports, sales, and promotional activities, for example, may give the young person with talent, ability, and desire an early break.

At first, it appears that the professional person also achieves his (or her) goal early in life. However, it is easy to forget that those who build careers in medicine, science, law, and the other professions must invest more time in their formal education. Physicians are often close to thirty when they start their practices. The same is true for lawyers, physicists, and other professionals.

Understanding plateau periods may help an ambitious employee do a better job of coping, but aren't there ways to shorten them? Yes, and the next chapter on motivating yourself should help you in this respect. The suggestions below will also deal with some specific possibilities.

Am I "using" my present role to improve my future whether or not I stay with the organization? Some people have the capacity to turn boring jobs into self-improvement periods. A good example might be the ambitious supervisor of a shipping operation who wants to know more about data processing. On company time she might start investigating the possibilities for her own department, thereby benefiting both her department and herself.

Am I taking advantage of all the training opportunities that are available to me now? Such opportunities could be both inside and outside the company walls. A "community involvement" of any kind can help one live through or even shorten a plateau period. Many employees have found "moonlighting" both therapeutic and advantageous in other ways.

Should I revise my present goals? Personal goal setting is dangerous, especially when it includes money rewards and time limits. You might want to change your "line of progression" to the top by asking for a horizontal transfer to a department where you could broaden your basic knowledge.

Have I applied for a promotion? Upward communication to let management know your "readiness" is often worth doing, even if nothing happens. It may not eliminate a plateau but it could shorten it.

Are there some company-sponsored activities I could become involved in? Often there are sports activities, study groups, and cultural programs that can give you additional employee and management contacts as well as pleasure. Such activities may not shorten plateau periods but they may make them *seem* shorter.

What about doing something spectacular? It is possible that you could volunteer for a very tough assignment that nobody else has been willing to tackle. This could provide you with a personal challenge. It could also communicate a great deal to upward management about your potential and "readiness" to accept more responsibility.

There are many other action steps people can take to shorten plateau periods or at least make them easier to live through. There are also cases where the employee should not live through them but rather adopt the zigzag route to the top and initiate a move to another organization. In contemplating such action please keep the following three points in mind.

1. The first years with an organization should be viewed by the new employee as training and apprenticeship years, as part of his (or her) total educational program. If the career employee receives a good salary and makes progress, he is doing very well indeed. The training and experience he is acquiring must be considered the plus factor during this period. The new employee is serving an internship something like that in the medical profession. All goals worth reaching for require some sacrifice.

2. Many new employees have received promotions before they were ready, and their careers have been permanently damaged. Will you be sufficiently trained for a good opportunity when it does come? Will you really be ready for the responsibility? Will you be sufficiently mature to handle it? "Too much too soon" is a real threat to your long-range goal.

3. Although few people question the fact that personal advancement is often slow during the starting years, they seldom point out that the tempo of personal progress can increase greatly in later years. This is one reason why the new worker should not set up a personal timetable for himself. Progress may be slow at the start of your career but very fast later. Set a goal for yourself, yes, but do not expect that goal to arrive exactly according to *your* time schedule. It may not fit that of your organization.

If you do set your own time schedule and management is unable to meet it, then you may lose your motivation to excel. This loss will hurt you as well as the company. The future of any company cannot be charted in detail many years in advance. Research, technical changes, market conditions, and many other factors are not predictable. Your job is to be ready when the opportunity occurs—ready and waiting.

Wearing a patience suit gracefully is not easy!

If you understand why you must wear it at times, you will have an advantage over others. And if you wear this suit well, the management suit may fit better when the time comes.

PROBLEM 16
Plateau

Lyle was the personnel director for a large banking organization. On his own, Lyle had been doing some quiet research for several months. His curiosity had been aroused over the high turnover of junior banking officers after they had been with the company about five years.

Upon investigation, Lyle learned that most trainees accepted on their informal training program reached their first supervisory position after just about two years. At this point most individuals became highly motivated and very productive. There was almost no turnover for a period of two or more years as they moved from one front-line supervisory position to a more demanding one, usually involving the supervision of more people and a salary increase.

But sooner or later each of these junior officers seemed to reach a plateau where no further promotions occurred for a long time. Further analysis showed that the plateau was caused by the difficulty these junior officers found in "breaking through" to middle-management roles.

In addition Lyle found that the typical growth pattern was to reach the top level of the first-line supervisory position in three to five years. At that point a temporary ceiling was reached and little more happened. Lyle called this period the *five-year plateau*. He soon discovered that his company was losing 60 percent of their junior-management people during the plateau period, when these people were waiting for middle-management roles to open up.

After interviewing several trainees who had already reached the plateau and a few who had already left the organization at that point, Lyle came to the following conclusions:

1. Most officers lost their patience with the firm before the plateau period ended.

2. Most seemed to be able to keep their positive attitudes for

about a year after reaching the plateau. But after that deterioration set in fast.

3. Because it was recognized that the company had an excellent training program, transferring to another bank was relatively easy. Furthermore, such a move could almost always be made at an increase in salary.

One individual made the following statement during an "exit" interview with Lyle. "It was great around here for the first three years. There was plenty to learn, promotions and salary increases were motivating, and the work was fulfilling. But once you reach that plateau it takes too much patience to wait around for the 'big jump.' At least I found it so."

If you were Lyle, what recommendations would you make to top management for either eliminating the plateau altogether or helping junior management people survive it? Be specific and fully justify your answers. (For a suggested answer, see page 199.)

17

Motivating
Yourself

"It is asking too much to suggest that people motivate themselves in the work environment. Motivation should come
from the supervisor, special rewards, or the job itself."

Many people would disagree with the above quotation. They
would claim that self-motivation is an absolute necessity in many
work environments. They would also claim that the more you can
learn about motivation the more you understand yourself and, as
a result, the more you will be in a position to inspire your own
efforts.

Let's assume that you find yourself in a job where things are
not going well. You feel stifled and "boxed in." You may, for
example, be much more capable than the job demands. Perhaps
too, the pay and benefits are only average, your immediate supervisor is difficult to deal with, and some other factors are not
ideal. Even so, you consider the organization a good one and you

"Hank's OK . . . he just needs motivation."

recognize that by earning promotions your long-term future can be excellent.

How can you inspire yourself to do a better-than-average job despite the temporary handicaps? How can you motivate yourself to live close to your potential despite a negative environment? How can you keep your attitude from showing? How can you keep from injuring important human relationships?

There are many theories or schools of thought on why people are motivated to achieve high productivity on the job. Most of these are studied by managers so that they will be in a better position to motivate the employees who work for them. In this chapter we are going to reverse the procedure. We are going to show you how to motivate yourself. *If your supervisor can be trained to motivate you why can't you learn to motivate yourself?*

Theory 1: Self-Image Psychology. This is frequently called the Psycho-Cybernetics School. The proponent of this theory is Dr. Maxwell Maltz, a plastic surgeon.* The basic idea is that in order to be properly motivated to achieve certain goals an individual must recognize the *need* for a good self-image. Dr. Maltz discovered in his work as a plastic surgeon that some patients became much more self-confident and far more motivated after having their faces greatly improved. Why? Maltz came to the conclusion that the image the individual had of himself (or herself) *inside* was more motivating than the changes he had made *outside*. In short, the way an individual *thinks* he or she looks can be more important than the way he or she actually looks to others.

How can you use this theory to motivate yourself?

Learn to picture yourself in a more complimentary way. First, research has shown that most people who have poor self-images actually *do* look better to others than they do to themselves. If this is true of you, you might try concentrating on your strong features instead of the weak ones, thus developing a more positive outlook and a better self-image.

Second, you might consider improving yourself on the outside as well as on the inside. You may not want to go as far as plastic surgery, but you could change your hairstyle, dress differently, lose or gain weight, exercise, and many other things. According to the theory, however, unless you recognize and accept the im-

---

*Maxwell Maltz, M.D., *Psycho-Cybernetics: The New Way to a Successful Life*, Prentice-Hall: Englewood Cliffs, N.J., 1960.

provement, nothing may happen. Psycho-cybernetics is, of course, a do-it-yourself project. You do all the work—and you get all the credit, too!

Grace is an example of what we are talking about. Without being aware that it happened, she permitted her visual image to deteriorate in an organization where grooming standards were high and important to career success. One day Grace had a conversation with a sensitive friend with whom she had an excellent relationship. She soon became aware that she was unmotivated and that, if it continued, her career would be stalled.

Grace decided to fight her negative feelings by paying more attention to cosmetics, by getting a new hairstyle, and by purchasing some new clothes. Did it work? In only a few weeks her friend said the improvement was exciting. More important, however, Grace herself knew she had restored her image. Once again she was motivated to achieve.

Theory 2: Maslow's Hierarchy of Needs. This is a very old theory developed by Abraham Maslow in his book *Motivation and Personality.*★ The premise here is that you have certain needs that must be fulfilled if you are to be properly motivated. These needs are built one on top of the other as in a pyramid.

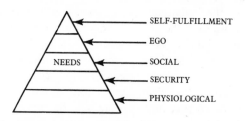

The bottom need is physiological—food, good health. The next is safety and security. The third from the bottom is social needs: one needs to be accepted and enjoy the company of others. Next are ego needs—recognition from others. Finally, at the pinnacle, is one's need for self-fulfillment or self-realization.

The crux of this theory is that the bottom needs must be fulfilled before the others come into play. In other words, you must satisfy your need for food and security *before* social needs become

---

★Abraham Maslow, *Motivation and Personality*, New York: Harper, 1954.

motivating. You must satisfy social and ego needs before self-fulfillment is possible.

How can you use this idea to motivate yourself to reach goals?

If you believe Maslow is right, it would be self-defeating to reverse the pyramid or "skip over" unsatisfied needs to reach others. Chances are good, however, that your first two needs are being adequately satisfied so you could make a greater effort to meet new people and make new friends. This could, in turn, help to satisfy your ego needs. With both your social and ego needs better satisfied you might be inspired to attempt greater creative efforts which could eventually lead you to greater self-realization.

It is possible that you feel it is foolish to worry about the lower needs when you have them pretty well satisfied. What you would want to do in this case is build more and better human relations to satisfy your social needs. That would in turn give you a big ego "push" and help you towards greater self-fulfillment. In short, you must believe in yourself if you are to reach any personal pinnacles. If you believe in yourself, the satisfaction of one need can give you the confidence to move on to another.

John, an M.B.A. with a highly innovative mind, had been dragging along for a year in a job that did not come close to using his potential. He knew he was not motivated but he couldn't figure out why. One of his close friends suggested that he needed more on-the-job recognition and that he should gamble with a dramatic move to gain the attention of top management.

John started looking around. Within three months he came up with a new, creative plan to solve a problem that management had been avoiding for years. Although the plan went through many revisions, John received the recognition he apparently needed. It was enough to remotivate him and get his career off dead-center.

Theory 3: Psychological Advantage. This school was founded by Saul W. Gellerman.* It contends that people constantly seek to serve their own self-interests, which change as they grow older. People can make their jobs work for them to give them a psychological advantage over other people at the same level. The way to create a psychological advantage in a starting job that is beneath your capacity is to learn all there is about that job. That

*Saul W. Gellerman, *Motivation and Productivity*, American Management Association, Inc., Vail-Ballou Press, 1963.

way, you can use the job as a springboard to something better, a position that will give you more freedom and responsibility. *How could you use this to inspire yourself?*

The best way, perhaps, is to be a little selfish about your job. Work for the organization and yourself at the same time. Instead of letting your job control you, perhaps pulling you and your attitude down, use it as a launching pad. Use it to build human relations that will be important later on. Study the structure of your organization so you will understand the lines-of-progression better than the other employees. Study the leadership style of your supervisor and others so that you will have a better one when your turn comes.

When you make full use of your present position you will be working more for yourself than you were. This, in turn, can motivate you to accomplish more for both yourself and the organization you work for. Here is an example.

Melinda's long-term goal was to become a fashion consultant for a major movie studio or television network, or possibly to become a fashion editor for a major metropolitan newspaper. Her short-term goal was to become a fashion buyer. When she finally became an assistant fashion buyer after four years with a major department store she thought she had arrived.

However, a year later she was still an assistant buyer with no additional prospects in sight. Melinda sensed that she was becoming demotivated. So she decided that as long as she was temporarily blocked from her immediate goal, she should use her present job to help her realize her long-term goal.

She then proceeded to use her job to get contacts with fashion experts in several fields. She availed herself of all opportunities to read fashion trends from company sources. She talked herself into opportunities to attend fashion clinics at company expense. Result? In a few short weeks she felt her motivation level returning to what it was.

Theory 4: Motivation-Hygienic School. This theory was developed by Professor Frederick Herzberg. Basically it claims that undesirable environmental factors (physical working conditions) can be dissatisfiers. Factors of achievement, recognition, and freedom, on the other hand, are satisfiers. All working environments have both negative and positive factors.

How can you take advantage of this theory?

People who maintain positive attitudes under difficult circumstances do so through attitude control. They concentrate *only* on the positive factors in their environment. You can, for instance, refuse to recognize the demotivating factors in your job and concentrate only on those things that will satisfy your needs better.

This could mean a deemphasis on physical factors and more emphasis on psychological factors such as social, ego, and self-fulfillment needs. One individual puts it this way: "I work in a very old building with poor facilities. Even so I have learned that I can be happy there because of the work I do and the great people I work with. One quickly gets used to fancy buildings and facilities and begins to take them for granted anyway."

Theory 5: The Maintenance-Motivation Theory. This school is much like Herzberg's hygienic approach and was developed by M. Scott Myers of Texas Instruments, Inc. His research found that employees usually fall into one of two groups: motivation seekers and maintenance seekers. In short, some people look for those factors that are motivating to them and are constantly pushing themselves toward fulfillment. Others are concerned with just staying where they are. Maintenance seekers spend much time talking about working conditions, wages, recreational programs, grievances, and similar matters and do little or nothing to motivate themselves. Motivation seekers, on the other hand, look beyond such matters.

How might you use this to improve your own motivation?

The obvious answer is, of course, to keep yourself out of the maintenance-seeker classification. To do this you should try not to overassociate with those in the maintenance classification. Without your knowing it, they could pull you into their camp. Try also to talk about positive things instead of being a complainer. Verbalizing negative factors often intensifies the dissatisfaction one feels. Turn your attention to things you can achieve on the job—not to the negative factors. The example below may help you understand the possibilities better.

It suddenly occurred to Rayford that he had become rather listless about a job that, six months ago, had seemed most promising. Why? Through self-evaluation he discovered that he was always talking about the negative aspects of his job, something he seldom did earlier. Had he permitted some of his negative co-workers to overinfluence him? Had he lost his positive focus on his job and career?

Although he could not pinpoint the cause, he decided it was

going to hurt his career if he didn't do something about it. Through pure self-discipline he forced his attention back to the positive factors about his job. He forced himself to talk about ways to improve or solve problems. He tried to divert conversations of co-workers into positive rather than negative channels.

It took a few weeks for him to do it but the results were encouraging. In explaining it to a superior he said this: "I either had to remotivate myself or look for another job."

The message of this chapter is that you need not change jobs when you find yourself on a plateau or in a somewhat negative work environment. You can employ various motivating techniques to pull yourself up to a management role where the situation is more satisfying. Instead of waiting for the organization itself to improve the situation, *you* can do something about it now.

PROBLEM 17
Options

After having worked for the same corporation for over three years, Norman decided that he had made a major mistake. He had been accepted on a formal management training program directly out of college. He had received his first supervisory role before his first year was up, but after that nothing else has happened. He had been on a plateau for over two years. In recent months he had been feeling extremely frustrated, stifled, and somewhat hostile. He admitted that his attitude was showing. He admitted that his personal productivity had leveled off.

Norman knew the primary reason for his lack of upward progress. His company had been going through a consolidation process and had put a freeze on new employees. Very few middle- and upper-management positions were opening up. Nevertheless, Norman finally came to the uncomfortable conclusion that he had to do something about it. He had to "force" some kind of action, even if it was difficult.

He then sat down and listed the advantages and disadvantages of his role with the company:

Advantages	Disadvantages
Good geographical location	Corporation not expanding
Good benefits	Salary only fair
Job security	Learning opportunities limited
Good personnel policies	Management overconservative
Good physical working conditions	Poor supervisor
Little commuting time	I have already made some human-relations mistakes
Good home neighborhood	Opportunities for upward communication with management limited
Enjoyable type of work	Fellow supervisors boring

After carefully going over the pros and cons of his job—and taking into consideration his three-year investment—Norman decided that he had the following options.

1. Go to the personnel department and discuss his frustration about being on a plateau.

2. Submit a written request for a transfer involving a promotion.

3. Start a serious search for a new job in a new company.

4. Resign with two weeks' notice and start looking for a new job.

5. Talk to his supervisor and ask for more responsibility.

6. Motivate himself so that management will recognize a change in attitude and consider him for the next promotion.

7. Relax, continue present efforts, and wait it out.

8. Motivate himself for three months. Then if nothing happens, resign.

9. After telling his boss, go to the president of the company with the problem.

10. Go to the president of the company to discuss his personal progress.

Assume you are Norman. First, make a list of the above options you would consider. Second, line them up in the order that you would undertake them. Third, add any action steps you would take that are not on the above list. Fourth, justify your decisions. (For a suggested answer, see page 200.)

18

Release
Your Frustrations
Harmlessly

This chapter has one simple goal and that is to introduce you to
the *frustration-aggression hypothesis*. It is an idea that can greatly
help you understand your own behavior as well as that of others.
Here is the story.

Everyone encounters frustrations in life. We learn to adjust to
most of them easily without hurting our relations with others.
Sometimes, however, a major frustration or a series of frustrations may cause our feelings to boil to the point where we lash
out verbally and seriously injure or destroy a relationship we
deeply treasure.

Naturally, there are many experiences that occur on the job

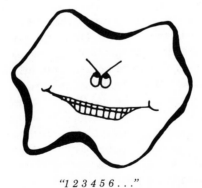

"1 2 3 4 5 6 . . ."

that are disturbing. In fact, most of your frustrations may be job-oriented. The typist who is in a hurry to get a letter on her (or his) boss's desk—and suddenly discovers she must change the ribbon in order to complete the letter—suffers a frustration. The mechanic who climbs under a car to do a repair job—only to discover that he (or she) took the wrong wrench with him—becomes frustrated. A supervisor who must get a report in before going home to an important dinner engagement can encounter a frustration.

A frustration is the inner feeling of disturbance or anxiety you experience when you meet a temporary block to your immediate goal.

The more important the goal is to you, the more intense is the disturbance. Major frustrations come about when something happens to keep you from reaching a goal that means a great deal to you. While small frustrations can usually be dealt with quickly, major frustrations must often be controlled for days or weeks until an adjustment can be made. This often means replacing one goal with another.

Now we must ask ourselves the big question: what happens when we become frustrated?

Almost always we become aggressive.

When a steam boiler builds up too much pressure inside, some of the steam must be released. If there is no safety valve, the boiler will explode. Just as the steam boiler must release some of the pressure after it reaches a certain point, so must the individual. This release comes usually in some form of aggressive behavior.

Take the case of the driver who becomes frustrated when he (or she) meets a slow-moving car on the highway. He may curse (verbal aggression) and drive on. Or he may pound his horn and speed around the slow car (physical aggression). Or it could disturb him so much that when he returns to his office he may not say hello to his secretary as would be his normal custom (silence).

Aggression takes many forms. Physical aggression, especially if it involves another person, is serious. It can be assault and battery and could mean a police record. Verbal aggression can also get a person into serious trouble. Telling off a fellow worker or supervisor at the wrong time and wrong place can destroy a relationship and cripple a person's progress.

The idea is to learn to release our aggression in acceptable ways.

There are acceptable forms of physical aggression. There are acceptable forms of verbal aggression.

A parent might become frustrated because of her (or his) small children. She could act out the aggression that follows the frustration by punishing one child with a very harsh slap in the face. This is an unacceptable release of aggression. On the other hand, if the parent released her aggression physically, by energetically washing windows, and then disciplined the child in some other manner, it would be more acceptable. This way the mother is taking out her aggression on the windows—not on the child.

There are many acceptable ways a person can release inner tensions due to frustration. Here are a few.

On the job	*Off the job*
Take a walk	Cook exotic foods
Talk things over with a third party	Clean out the garage
	Play golf or go bowling
Do some disagreeable stock work	

Sometimes just by doing something physical we release inner tensions and no one is hurt. It is usually more difficult to find acceptable ways to release inner tensions on the job than it is off the job.

If a worker became frustrated on the job and picked a fight with a fellow worker, this would be an unacceptable release of aggression. If, on the other hand, he (or she) released his aggressions by walking away and slamming a door where nobody could hear it, he would be releasing his aggression in an acceptable manner. He *could* hurt his human relationships, however, by slamming a door in *front* of others. They might interpret the action as a display of temper or immaturity.

As a mature, mentally healthy person, you must seek and find acceptable releases for your inner aggression. You should conduct yourself in such a manner as to eliminate many of the frustrations of life. The fewer frustrations you have, the fewer times you will have to seek acceptable releases.

But you cannot eliminate all frustrations from life. You should expect to find it necessary to release your anxiety feelings occasionally. It is not always healthy for a person to keep his or her inner tensions bottled up inside. Some release is necessary and healthy.

After a frustrating experience on the job, it is easy to release inner tensions by saying the wrong thing. People who say things that are upsetting to others may be guilty of verbal aggression. They may be saying these things because they have suffered a frustration or series of frustrations and this is a form of release. Their inner tensions, caused by a series of frustrations, have reached the boiling point.

Sometimes a succession of frustrations causes a more serious inner buildup of pressure. When this happens, some verbal release is necessary. You will do well, however, to refrain from this kind of verbal release to someone on the job. It would be wiser to unburden yourself to someone you can trust outside the organization—your spouse or a good friend.

Here is an illustration that will help you to understand the importance of the frustration-aggression hypothesis.

Alice was intelligent, highly motivated, and well educated. She joined a large utility company as a receptionist. She liked her job, and for two years her productivity and human relations were very good. She took advantage of every opportunity to learn. She received four salary increases.

One day, in talking to the personnel director, she mentioned that she would like to qualify as an employment interviewer. The personnel director, pleased with her success so far, encouraged her. He told Alice that she would be considered if an opportunity came along. Alice, more highly motivated than ever, continued to do an outstanding job and set her goal for the next opening in the personnel department.

Two weeks later another person was promoted to the personnel department as an interviewer. Alice was not informed about the change. Not thinking that the plans for this personnel change might have been set before her initial talk with the personnel director, Alice permitted herself to become deeply frustrated. She had set a goal for herself and now they had selected another person.

"At least they could have talked to me!"

"Why should that person get the breaks?"

"So that's the way they keep their promises!"

Alice, without thinking it through, permitted her frustration to grow. Indeed, she set out to feed it, for talking it over with a few fellow employees only intensified her feelings.

What happened?

Alice released her frustration through verbal aggression. For the first time in her career, she sounded off in a highly emotional manner at a weekly staff meeting. She voiced more than her share of gripes during coffee breaks. And all of this found its way back to the personnel department. What was the result? What you might expect: Alice, through her verbal aggression, hurt herself. Six months later another position was open in personnel and Alice was passed over.

What should she have done?

Alice should have released her aggressive behavior outside her job until she discovered the truth of the situation. She could have spent more time playing her favorite sport or talking her problem over with a close friend. Or she could have put it into writing. This seems to help a number of people. None of these actions would have hurt anyone. After releasing some of her inner feelings of hostility away from work Alice could have become more objective and realized she was in error.

We must all learn to live with frustrating experiences without becoming verbally aggressive on the job, without damaging our relations with others.

Aggressive behavior coming from inner disturbances and hostilities takes many strange forms. It's not always physical or verbal. In extreme cases, aggression takes the form of silence. Deliberate silence. Planned silence.

Silence on the part of the person who has been frustrated is a most potent weapon. Nothing is more uncomfortable to your fellow workers than your silence. No one can interpret your silence. All anyone can do is leave you alone and wait. But it is uncomfortable for them, and productivity suffers.

When a person takes out his or her inner aggressive feelings in silence, who is at the receiving end? Fellow employees? The supervisor? Although everyone suffers from silence of this nature, the silent person himself suffers the most. He is, in fact, taking out his aggressive feelings on himself. Naturally, this is most destructive to the human personality. It is also juvenile. Many normal, mature people, however, temporarily react to a series of frustrations in this manner.

It is hoped that the preceding discussion has given the reader a good understanding of the frustration-aggression hypothesis. To summarize, how can you put this idea to work for you?

1. If you really understand the idea, you will admit that your frustrations often produce aggressive behavior of some kind and you should learn to recognize this. With this recognition should come the ability to channel aggressive actions into acceptable outlets. Be careful to release your aggressions in the right way and in the right place. Keep from releasing them on the job in a way that will hurt your future.

2. You should be able to recognize aggressive behavior in others (including executives). This should help you remember that aggressive action by others is usually not directed toward you personally. You may just happen to be at the wrong place at the wrong time and the best available target for the verbal abuse. You should try to accept such behavior as a natural outcome of uncontrollable frustrations and not overreact to it. This attitude should make for better human understanding.

3. You should be more sensitive to verbal aggression on your own part and be very cautious in group discussions and staff meetings. When you need to release feelings verbally, do so to a friend outside the company and not to a fellow employee.

4. You should not let aggressive behavior keep you from reaching your ultimate goal. When a detour is necessary, you should take it. When an unexpected block to your plans appears, accept it for what it is. If frustration occurs, release it in acceptable ways and come up with an alternate goal. Do not allow aggressive behavior to hinder your future.

There is another form of aggression that should be mentioned. It is subtle and sinister and has been the downfall of many career-minded persons. It is aggression on the part of an employee toward the company he or she works for. There is rarely anything personal about such a person's aggressive behavior. Such a person seems to get along well enough with his fellow workers and immediate supervisors.

Instead, his aggression always seems to be directed toward the company itself. It isn't just the top brass or middle management. It is the company. He often seems to hold his present plight (lack of progress or of personal adjustment to life) against the company.

In a very real sense it *is* frustrating to work inside any organization. Some rules must be followed. Some degree of conformity is expected. Some loss of individuality is usually necessary. Some people, however, seem to nurse their minor frustrations into one major hang-up against the organization itself. When this is permitted to happen, aggressive action of serious proportions frequently develops. The employee begins to fight a hypothetical monster that seems to be controlling his life without giving him a chance to change. Often one hears expressions like these from such an individual:

"This outfit does nothing but chew people up and spit them out."

"This company is so large that the only thing that keeps us from getting lost altogether is the payroll department."

"I'd put in for a transfer but by the time it got through channels I'd be ready to retire."

It is counterproductive to direct one's aggressive behavior toward a large corporate structure. In the first place, these organizations are usually too large. Second, when a person attacks his company he starts to lose his loyalty to it. *And it begins to show.* Not overnight, of course, but in subtle ways that begin to hurt that person's progress in the company.

This chapter has attempted to show you why you should try to release your frustrations harmlessly. Its purpose has been to help you maintain positive relationships with those who work around you so that your career success will be enhanced.

PROBLEM 18
Frustration

It took Victor three months to make up his mind to switch to the new company. His decision to do so was based primarily upon the promise that they would push him ahead as fast as possible. In his opinion his previous firms had never given him the opportunity to move ahead at a pace that was satisfying to him.

Everything went well until he discovered that an engineer, less experienced than he, had been promoted. This caused him to wonder whether he had been oversold on the opportunities that were available for him.

Shortly before Vic had completed six months with the company, he was asked if he would accept a transfer to another plant some 200 miles away. He accepted and became very excited because he thought it would eventually mean a big promotion for him. On reporting to work at the new plant, however, he discovered he had little more responsibility than the one he had left. There was no discussion of a pay increase. Having built up his hopes, Vic felt let down.

Then other things happened. He soon learned that his living expenses were higher in the new location. His wife told him that the schools there were not as good. One negative thing after another happened until Vic became increasingly frustrated. One afternoon after two weeks in the new assignment, he walked into the personnel department and explosively released his pent-up feelings.

Halfway through the outburst the personnel officer said, "Slow down. Take it easy. Cool off. Relax." Then he proceeded to read a letter just received from the home office announcing that Vic was to replace a man who had just received a promotion himself. It was a big jump.

Was Vic justified in his outburst? What might he have done to prevent it? Did he harm himself permanently, even though he did receive the promotion? (For a suggested answer, see page 201.)

19

Meet Joe Harvey Again

We met Joe in an earlier chapter. Here he is again, with some new questions.

How can I keep a positive attitude when my job is frequently boring?

People are usually bored for either of two reasons. First, there may be little or no activity connected with the job. Business may slow down or the work load may drop temporarily. Second, the work itself may be boring. This is especially true of jobs that are repetitive or routine—jobs that rarely offer a new challenge.

In the case of inactivity, the employee must manufacture work in order to keep a positive attitude. He (or she) must use his initiative to find work—*any* work—during slow periods. Inactivity on the job will always give a person a negative attitude. The only way to fight it, Joe, is to find something constructive to do.

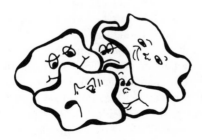

"Yes, I know, but . . ."

The matter of having a job that is not consistently challenging is another kind of problem. People who have lived through boring jobs claim that they have had to *make* their jobs interesting. They experiment with doing the job in different ways. They play games with themselves to keep up their interest. In other words, they look at the positive side of the job.

Boredom is a sinister emotion. It can destroy your positive attitude and sap your enthusiasm without your knowing it. Because this can be very unhealthy, challenge yourself from the very start. If you do this, boredom will not become a major problem and you will keep the positive attitude you started out with.

Whom should I turn to if I run into a human-relations problem I can't handle myself?

If you have analyzed the problem carefully and made repeated attempts to solve it yourself, there are many people you can turn to for assistance. The important thing is that you go to *somebody*, Joe. You must talk these problems over and not keep them inside until they grow out of proportion and eventually damage your career. Time itself does not always solve human problems. When your productivity and that of others are being impaired, action is imperative.

Usually your immediate supervisor is the person to see. In some cases, someone in the personnel department might be better. It is important to go to someone whom you respect and who is receptive. It is also important to go to someone who will discuss the problem in confidence. If there is no one inside the company you honestly feel you can consult, you will have to talk with an outsider. But be sure the person will keep the problem under his (or her) hat.

In discussing your problem remember that it is always better not to identify personalities. Try to present the problem in a fair and objective manner without building too much of a case for yourself. Remember, Joe, that it takes two to create a human-relations problem. Seldom is any problem entirely the fault of *one* person. Talking over a problem with the right person may not solve it, but it can give you a perspective on your problem. It can lower the pressure that has been building and give you some new insights into human understanding.

What do you do when you feel your immediate supervisor is strongly prejudiced against you?

If you have been harassed or unfairly treated over an extended period of time—and you are absolutely certain that some form of prejudice exists—you should take the following three steps, in sequence.

1. Arrange a face-to-face discussion in private with your supervisor as soon as possible. State your feelings openly and frankly. Don't accuse him (or her) or needlessly antagonize him by your attitude or words. Stress his behavior and not him as a person. Once you have stated your case, listen carefully to his side of the story. Should he disclaim any feelings of prejudice toward you, accept him at his word and do your level best to improve the relationship during the next few weeks.

2. If the relationship does not improve in the next few weeks, go to your personnel officer or to your supervisor's boss and request a two- or three-way discussion—including the supervisor. As in your previous confrontation, state your case to the best of your ability and continue to be a good listener. Whatever happens as a result of this meeting, try not to be hostile or vindictive toward the supervisor or the company.

3. If the relationship still does not improve and the harassment and unfair treatment continues, formally request a transfer and at the same time start looking for a position with another company. There is no reason why you should continue to work under a supervisor guilty of prejudice toward you, Joe.

How do you get through to someone who is insensitive to human relations?

Everyone is insensitive to human relations at times. In rare instances, it might be possible for you to help a close friend or co-worker build better relationships with others, *if he (or she) wants your help.*

This is a risky business, however, and should usually be left to professional counselors. The cause may be deeper than you think. Your best approach in these situations is to be satisfied in building the best possible relationship with them even though they may not respond as you feel they should. Not all people, of course, can be helped even by the professionals.

Can a person be formally trained to be more sensitive to the needs of others?

A great deal of experimental work is going on today in this area. Many different kinds of sensitivity and encounter groups are being conducted. Whether such sessions are helpful or harmful to the individual depends on many complicated factors. The most important, factor is the professional background, skill, and sensitivity of the group's leader. Check to see whether or not a group is sponsored by a reliable organization and conducted by a truly professional person. Also take into consideration your own feelings. If the idea of an encounter group is too threatening, you would be wise not to join one.

What if I should get stuck in an assignment with no future? How do I go about getting a transfer?

Every organization has its own procedure, Joe. You must always respect local ground rules. Most transfers are handled through personnel departments. A request for a transfer should go through normal channels and, if possible, should be made on a face-to-face basis with or without a written statement.

It is never human-relations smart to act prematurely on transfer requests. If you do, you might communicate to others that you can't handle the job or that you can't take a difficult temporary assignment. Some starting jobs, for example, are traditional stages in a career, and everyone must sweat them out. Under these conditions, an early request can hurt you.

What action should I take if I find myself in a position for which I am overqualified?

It is not unusual for a very bright or highly educated person to start a career from an entry position that does not come close to fully using his or her potential. In such a situation, it is usually to the individual's advantage to live with the job—do it well and keep a positive attitude—until something more challenging opens up. If you find yourself in such a position. Joe, there are two factors you should keep in mind.

1. Don't communicate to others, through your attitude, that you feel you are too good for the job. You could damage your

relations with people and perhaps postpone the day when you will receive more of a challenge.

2. Your best approach is to try and make your job better than it now is. In other words, assume more responsibility as opportunities arise. Without hurting your relationships with others, demonstrate your ability in different ways. You could, for example forward well-researched suggestions through the proper channels, or ask to make certain improvements in procedures, or simply do something others have neglected. If you take this approach you will keep management aware of your potential in a positive way. Chances will then be good that they will make better use of your potential sooner.

Should you find yourself inside an organization that cannot make good use of your special potential, you should make a switch as soon as possible. A job that temporarily doesn't use your potential is one thing. A company that can't use it is another. Don't be afraid to quit a job if it is wrong for you. Too many people stay with a job they got by accident during a period of need.

When and how should I go about asking for a raise or a salary adjustment?

Salary hang-ups between an employee and management can create difficult situations. But don't start out anticipating any problems. It may never be necessary for you to ask for a raise or adjustment. The great majority of raises are made without request.

There are circumstances, however, when action on your part might be necessary and advisable, Joe. For example, you might have been promised an increase that did not materialize on time. A pleasant reminder could quickly clear up the oversight.

You might also find yourself in the position where you are doing the same job as others but your pay is less. Or you have waited longer than others have for an increase. Or your job needs to be reclassified. If this is so, you should do something about it. But don't jump too fast with too little. Do you have the facts straight? Have you fully demonstrated your superior productivity over a substantial period of time? Has your responsibility really increased? Are there other factors involved?

Don't be afraid of going to management to discuss your salary problems. If it is important to you, it is also important to them. The longer you wait and nurse the problem, the more disturbed and negative you will become. *Salary problems destroy positive attitudes and productivity and must be reconciled as soon as possible.*

But go about it in the right way to avoid making a serious human-relations mistake. Try not to carry a chip on your shoulder. Try not to build a case for yourself ahead of time. Listen to the other side.

A salary discussion, like other discussions, should provide two-way communication that will solve the problem. It should not be a bargaining session in which deep hostilities develop —hostilities that are often irreconcilable. After all, your goal should be to get a fair adjustment and at the same time not injure your relations with management.

Why do we need good human relations with people we may never see again and who therefore can't help us in business?

There are two basic reasons why you should practice good human relations with *everybody* you meet, both on and off the job, Joe. The first reason is philosophical; the second, practical. First, practicing good human relations should become a way of life. It is not something you should turn on or off based upon what it can do for you. You must believe that everybody you meet is important and worth the best treatment you can provide. Unless you really feel this way, though, you are only playing a game. Your human-relations endeavors will most likely be interpeted as surface gestures. As a result, your relationships with others will be very shallow.

Second, you never can tell whether or not you will meet another person again. People have a way of showing up in strange places. If you mistreat or ignore a person when you first meet him (or her), this individual may make it difficult for you later on when you do need him.

If you are practicing good human relations but your supervisor is not, how do you cope?

Chances are good you won't be stuck with such a supervisor

for long, so view your experience as temporary. Almost everyone in upper management has had to endure a difficult supervisor at some point. Don't allow the situation to force you to resort to poor human-relations practice yourself, though. Try to build a good human-relations reputation despite your uncomfortable situation.

Study the mistakes your supervisor makes. Make sure you don't someday incorporate them into your own leadership style. You should also be generous enough to keep in mind that being a supervisor is probably more difficult than you suspect. When you get there, you may not be as good a manager as you think.

How do you maintain good human relations when trying to rebuff advances from a member of the opposite sex who is in your department —especially if it is your supervisor?

Be gracious but firm in front of others in the department. You might not only build better relations, but you might solve the problem itself.

How can you build good horizontal relations with others when they know you are a good personal friend of the manager because of a previous relationship?

It is a tough thing to live through, but the following will help. (1) Keep your relations with this person on a strict business basis while on the job. (2) Do not take advantage of the relationship in any manner or form. Concentrate on keeping your personal productivity above reproach. (3) Work harder at your horizontal relationships so that your co-workers will eventually respect you for yourself and your contribution—and not because you know the manager personally.

How do you handle a situation in which two of your co-workers have a very strong dislike for each other, and you are in the middle?

Stay in the middle and do the best you can. Both relationships are equally important to you and to the productivity of the department. You must try not to side with one or the other and contribute to a possible split in the department. Your best bet is to try to keep both relationships strong and healthy.

If you side with one person you automatically hurt your relationship with the other. It is also possible that the person you side with may resign and leave you holding the bag, or the person you turn away from may become your supervisor. There is nothing to keep you from trying to resolve the problem, but you should understand the risks involved. Remember that your supervisor probably knows what is going on and can take action from a better position than yours.

What if I should discover a fellow employee being dishonest? What responsibility do I have to the company?

Your company may have a policy you should follow, Joe. In any case, you do have a responsibility to your company and to yourself to report such behavior.

One possible procedure is to go to the employee directly and tell him or her that you noticed a certain incident, and that you will feel obliged to go to management should you observe such an incident again. This is not easy to do. You must be careful of your facts. You should never accuse. Just say that you observed.

If this approach seems inadvisable, your only alternative is to report the incident to a responsible person who will honor your confidence and start an investigation. Whatever happens after that is not your responsibility.

Dishonesty is a touchy business. You must protect yourself from involvement and at the same time carry out your responsibility as an employee. An on-the-spot accusation should be avoided at all costs. Evidence is hard to come by, and getting it should be left to the experts.

I expect to be promoted to supervisor in my department soon. How should I handle the problem of supervising my close friends who are now my co-workers?

There are three things to keep in mind when you make this transition. First, it will be necessary to set your discipline line early and firmly so that everyone will know that you have the leadership ability to be a supervisor and that you will not be intimidated. Second, you must refuse to play favorites because it would quickly destroy some relationships. Third, talk the problem over with your co-worker friends. Simply tell them that they will have to understand your new role. Ask them how they might handle it if they were in your place. Your transition into management might also mean a change in your off-duty relationships with some previous co-worker friends. If so, it is the price you must pay to succeed in your new role.

Do I have a public-relations responsibility to my company?

The image your company has in the mind of the public has a great influence on the company's success. So the answer to your question is yes. Of course, if you have contact with customers, public relations is part of your job. You are paid to work well with customers. But even if you have no on-the-job contacts with the public, you still have a public-relations responsibility. The image of your company can be hurt around the bridge table, on the golf course, or through many other contacts you may have.

Certain problems and discussions should be kept within the company family. As long as you accept employment with a company, you are an insider and you share in the responsibility to communicate a good image to outsiders. It is *your* company. If you downgrade it in any way to your friends, you are in effect downgrading yourself.

Is too much conformity demanded in a large organization? Must I lose my individuality to build a career?

A certain amount of conformity is definitely necessary in working for a company. But isn't this also true of our culture in general? Isn't it true, at least to some extent, in community life? Isn't it also true in social organizations?

Remember the chapters in the book that dealt with building good horizontal and vertical working relationships? You will recall it was suggested that some degree of conformity would be necessary. *Some* conformity does not mean you will lose your whole identity. Your company does not want you to become a carbon copy of other people. It does not want you to become a face in the crowd. You will lose some of your value to the company if you do.

It is important that you become a good working member of

the company and still keep your individuality. The most basic of all human-relations principles is recognition of individual differences. Overconformity is as unacceptable as nonconformity. The line between is a tightrope all employees walk. To be a strong working member of a group and still maintain one's individuality is no easy trick.

Variety and diversity are helpful in most group situations. The strongest team is often a group of people *not* with the same talents and same weaknesses but with a variety of each. The wise leader attempts to surround himself (or herself) not with people exactly like himself but people who are different and can therefore contribute more to his leadership.

PROBLEM 19
Hostility

Lupe was a self-confident, sophisticated woman with a high potential. She recently took a job working under four editors at a large publishing concern. Her position was classified as a general office clerk and typist. The pay was good. The hours and location were great.

Everything went beautifully for a while. Everyone admitted Lupe was a superior employee. It wasn't long, however, before three things began to bother her. First, the job itself was boring. It was all too routine and just did not challenge her enough. Second, she was certain she could do a better job of editing than some of the editors.

She also thought she could get along well with the art department, coming up with creative ideas to improve manuscripts, and many other things that only editors were in a position to do. Third, she could sense the hostility coming from a few of the other women around the office, especially from one of the editors she worked for.

What kind of human-relations mistakes might Lupe have made? What would have made it possible for her to move into a more challenging position with the blessings and support of the other people in her department? (For a suggested answer, see page 202.)

20

When Other Pastures Look Greener

Freedom to accept or resign a job, seek employment in a certain field, or join an organization of one's choice is an important right. It should be appreciated by all free people. But what does it really mean to you?

It means that you can leave a position with a large or small organization and go into business for yourself. It means you can leave your occupation and go back to school to continue your education. It means you can leave one company and join another. It means you can follow the zigzag route to the top by making a move to another organization every time you can substantially improve your future. It means you can keep on leaving one com-

"Things always look better on the outside."

pany for another until you find the job, occupational area, or company that's right for you.

Some resignations are soundly planned and are best for the organization and the individual. Some resignations, for a variety of personal reasons, are unavoidable. Some, however, seem to stem from poor judgment and turn out to be mistakes.

There are dangers to any resignation. You could wind up with a job that is not as good as the one you left. You might even wind up temporarily stranded. Thousands of people leave organizations every year only to regret it later. The pastures in another occupational area or company may, from a distance, look greener than they really are. Resigning a position, whether you have a door open elsewhere or not, is a serious step.

When, then, should you resign a position?

As a general rule, you should resign when you have been *unhappy and unproductive for a considerable length of time.* Under such conditions your career with the company has already been seriously damaged. A new start in a new environment would most likely be to your advantage.

Young people who are ambitious should look elsewhere for employment when they discover they have not been working close to their potential for a long time. They should seek opportunities elsewhere when their productivity has been down for months, and they can't get it back up. They should consider other options when their attitude has been negative for a long time and they do not seem to be able to do anything about it.

Surveys and statistics show, however, that most resignations are not due to the above reasons, *but are based primarily upon personality conflicts and human problems.* Because such problems can frequently be solved or at least made less traumatic, it would appear that many people resign their positions for the wrong reasons. In other words, leaving a job because it is not the *right* one for you is one thing. Leaving a job because of human problems that you might solve or continue to find elsewhere is something else.

To help you avoid these and other mistakes, here are some questions to ask yourself when considering a resignation.

Are you resigning under emotional stress?

We are all tempted to chuck a job when everything seems to be going wrong or when we are deeply frustrated and emotionally upset. It is a natural reaction. A resignation, however, should be a rational decision based upon many facts, and should be made only after long, careful analysis and planning.

It is difficult to think clearly and logically when you are emotionally disturbed about a problem that cannot be quickly solved. During these periods, back away from such a serious decision. Sleep on it. Talk to a third person. Give it time. A resignation should not be an impulsive decision. In the majority of cases it is irrevocable.

Have you talked your situation over with your supervisor or the person who hired you?

Many employees are fearful of talking over a possible resignation with a management person. Some people believe they will be terminated immediately if they voice their dissatisfaction. They feel that their chances of finding a better job elsewhere would be weakened. Some feel it would be an act of disloyalty. Others feel it to be a waste of time.

Whatever your reason, you would be wise not to resign until *after* you have discussed the problem with your supervisor or someone in personnel. A twenty-minute discussion with the right person has stopped many a foolish resignation. Many problems can be resolved through free and open communication with management. Give those in charge a chance to resolve your problem before you take final action. You have nothing to lose. You could even discover that the position you are thinking of leaving has more potential than any you could find elsewhere.

Are you resigning because of a personality conflict?

Resigning because of a single personality is no way to build a lifelong career. This is not to say that such conflicts cannot be serious. They can be. But they can usually be resolved with time and effort. Give someone in authority a chance to help. Give time a chance to help. Most of all, be honest with yourself and ask whether you can afford to let one person destroy a promising career—especially when it is *yours*.

Are you resigning to save face?

Everyone makes mistakes. Sometimes you may overcommit yourself or take a stand on an issue that you feel you cannot back away from. Resigning on this basis can be a mistake, especially if you have exaggerated the difficulty of the adjustment. It may be better to admit a mistake than to pay a price out of all proportion. Such a resignation might be harmful to both your future and the company's.

Are you living close to your potential?

Your future depends on your having a position in a company where you can work close to your potential. If the gap between what you are capable of doing and your current level of productivity is too wide, your career progress may be stalled. You must be able to use your ability, aptitude, and talent to a reasonable extent. You must be productive to succeed. You must find a way to contribute.

Your company is entitled to the best you. If you find your position doesn't bring out the best in you, then it isn't fair to either you or the company for you to remain. You should find something more suitable. An employee who is not productive is doing herself (or himself) and her company more harm than good.

If after serious consideration of all the above questions you decide to resign in the best interests of both parties, how should you go about it? Here are a few tips on how to resign gracefully.

Resign on a face-to-face basis. Always go to the person who hired you as well as to your supervisor and resign face to face. A letter of resignation or a telephone resignation alone will always leave a bad impression. It may hurt you later on when another organization wants a reference. You will gain the respect of management when you resign in person. You will feel better too.

Tell management the real reasons for your resignation. It may be difficult for you to reveal the actual causes for your leaving but you should do so anyway. Reliable information of this kind can lead to changes that will benefit those you leave behind.

If you are honest with management, they will understand you better and your status as a former employee will be improved. Honesty is always the best human-relations policy.

Give ample notice. Be sure that you give at least the traditional two weeks' notice. This amount of time may be necessary for the company to recruit and train a replacement.

Continue to be productive. Don't take advantage of the fact that you are leaving. You will gain respect from others as well as personal satisfaction by working hard up to the very last hour. This is one way to leave a clean record behind you.

Turn in all equipment. All company equipment, down to the most minute item, should be officially turned in through regular channels.

Transfer all responsibilities to your replacement gracefully. Give the person taking over your job a break. Give her (or him) all possible help and assistance. Try not to leave her with any problems you can take care of before leaving. Transfer to her as far as possible any good relationships you have developed.

Swallow any last-minute negative comments. There is a temptation for some people to become negative and pour out their hostilities after they have turned in their resignation. It is especially important not to transfer your negative attitudes to your replacement. Give her a chance to make her own adjustment without sour notes from you.

Say good-bye when you go. Be courteous enough to say good-bye personally to all the people who have helped you. If you are unable to see someone, send her (or him) a note.

Always resign a position in such a manner that you will feel free to seek reemployment there at a later date. You are the sum total of all your experiences. When you leave a job, you do not leave empty-handed. You take your experience and training with you. And you take the knowledge you've gained from all your human-relations experiences. Such knowledge is never without value. Make that known. Leave on the right foot.

In closing, it should also be mentioned that business and governmental organizations sometimes find it necessary to terminate the services of some employees due to circumstances beyond their control. Most business organizations must adjust quickly to economic and social changes. This sometimes means organizational shake-ups that eliminate certain roles.

A young shopping-center manager recently made this statement: "One of the most important things I learned in college was to anticipate and be willing to accept change. I expected I would walk into a dynamic, changing world—I was not prepared for the world as it really is today. The changes that I see around me as far as personnel are concerned are enough to blow your mind."

Because of such changes, there is a possibility that you may someday be involved in a layoff, cutback, or furlough situation. Here are three more tips that might help you during such an adjustment period.

1. Remember that your layoff is not really the company's fault. Nor is it yours. So it is a waste of time to blame anyone for it.

2. It does not hurt your reputation to be caught in such a situation. You can and should continue to be proud of your record.

3. It is discouraging enough to lose your job. If you lose your positive attitude along with it, you are a double loser. Maintain a positive attitude. Go out and find yourself a more rewarding position.

PROBLEM 20
Interview

Mark was deeply discouraged for two reasons. One, his present job was intolerable. Second, he had had seven job interviews in the past three months but he had received little positive response to any and no job offers.

Mark felt his discouragement was justified. He had been trying extremely hard and had followed sound job-seeking practices. He had done advance research on all organizations ahead of the interview. He was meticulous in his grooming. He was careful in completing the application blank and always made certain to submit a résumé along with it. In addition to all this, it was clear that he had more than minimum qualifications for all positions for which he applied.

What was wrong?

Mark decided to discuss his problem with a very perceptive placement director. Together they came to the conclusion that Mark was not "coming through" or transmitting his "best attitude" during the interview period. In other words, he was losing out to other applicants because he was not communicating well. Were his answers to questions too low-key? Or too brief? Was he overnervous? What might he do to "sell himself" to the interviewers without overdoing it and coming on too strong?

Because you made a successful transfer recently—with a substantial increase in pay and responsibility—Mark comes to you for assistance. He asks you four typical questions, ones that he has been encountering in his interviews. He wants to measure the way you handle them and make comparisons to his own responses. He wants to model his replies after yours. This will, in turn, improve his personal confidence and help him communicate his true worth as a prospective employee.

Because Mark is a good friend you agree to do this. Now, in order to provide the maximum assistance you agree to do one of the following:

1. Actually role play the situation and reply to the questions below in class to the best of your ability. Assume all other factors

(application, grooming, and so forth) are up to standard and that you are *fully* qualified for the hypothetical position.

2. Write out, word for word, the way you would reply to each question below.

a. What made you decide you would like to work for our company?

b. What do you feel you will be able to contribute to our organization?

c. What human-relations skills will you bring with you?

d. Why have you decided to leave your present organization?

(For a discussion of this problem, see page 202.)

Suggested Answers to Case Problems

The human-relations problems presented at the end of each chapter in this book were designed to be springboards for individual thinking and discussion purposes. There are no exact answers to any of the problems.

In the first place, only the most essential facts of each problem are outlined. It is therefore impossible to give definite or complete answers to any problem. Without *all* the facts, anything approaching a definite or complete answer would be dangerous indeed. Also, different points of view are always possible (even encouraged) in discussions of human-relations problems.

The following so-called answers, then, are nothing more than the author's opinion of how he would approach the problem with the available facts. They should serve only as a guide to the independent thinking of the reader and the discussion leader.

PROBLEM 1
Reality

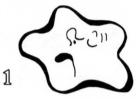

"It's <u>who</u> you know that counts."

It is easy to understand why Rod was disturbed when the other two received promotions ahead of him. His pride was hurt because he had worked hard and efficiently at his job. But there is at least some evidence that Rod was trying to escape his full human-relations responsibility. Did he make enough effort to cooperate and build good relationships with his co-workers? Was he sufficiently tolerant? Did he put everything into personal efficiency and nothing into human relations?

The author believes that Rod was not fully justified in saying, "It isn't what you know but who you know that counts." It appears that Rod was trying to rationalize his unwillingness to build better relationships. He was reminded twice by his supervisor to be more a part of the group. He did not take the hint. It would therefore appear that Rod felt his job depended much more on his personal productivity than on his human-relations skill. He did not see why he had more of a responsibility to work closely with others in his department in order to help *their* productivity.

Rod's case shows that an ambitious employee who works hard and efficiently does not necessarily live up to minimum human-relations standards. Rod should develop a better balance between productivity and human skills if he is to contribute more to the department and to his own future career.

PROBLEM 2
Adjustment

"What's wrong with my personality?"

George would probably have to make some concessions before he found another job where he would be happy. He failed to understand that when he was aloof, distant, and hostile he was uncomfortable to work next to. He failed to comprehend that his fellow workers might have needed to communicate with him on a friendly basis whether he needed to communicate with them or not.

George must learn to relax and give more of himself if he wants an environment in which he can be happy and productive. He will never make his maximum contribution to his job and company if he stays so deeply inside his shell and expects others to come to him.

George may be extremely sensitive about going halfway in building relationships because he was rejected or hurt in the past. If he made a new effort to discover that most people are not only easy to know but *worth* knowing, he would have confidence and adjust more easily to all new environments.

There is no evidence that George's supervisor took the time to get to know him and help him make a satisfactory adjustment. It is possible that the supervisor did not live up to his (or her) full responsibility. But on the other hand, many demands are put on front-line managers. The new employee must sometimes accept primary responsibility for making her (or his) own initial adjustment.

PROBLEM 3
Attitude

"It's hard to stay positive."

It is very difficult to pinpoint the very day when a major change in attitude takes place. It would therefore be a hasty judgment to agree with Manuel that he should have resigned his job a year ago. Of course, now that it is over, Manuel has the benefit of hindsight to help him assess his unhappy experience.

Although changes in attitude usually creep up on a person rather slowly, Manuel should have tested himself when he discovered that his enthusiasm was down over a period of a few weeks. Was it the job itself that was responsible? Was it a conflict over his own personal career desires? Was it his own immaturity? Manuel should have taken an honest inventory of himself and his job much earlier. He should have talked to his manager or perhaps a professional counselor.

If he came to the conclusion that his values and desires were not sufficiently in harmony with the job, he should have started to look elsewhere or considered going back to school. If, however, the job itself was not the major cause of his negative attitude, then he should have made more of an effort to regain his positive attitude.

More and more graduates are forced to accept secondary career choices due to poor career planning and an even poorer job market. Most seem able to adjust without becoming overnegative. A few even discover that their second or third choices were even better than their first. Those who remain unhappy should find more harmonious work or return to school for training in a new career area. Employees who remain negative over a long period hurt their career possibilities.

PROBLEM 4
Decision

"My supervisor ignores me."

Bernie should get good results from his approach, providing he stays with it long enough. It is fortunate that he did not decide to concentrate exclusively on horizontal relationships. No matter how unapproachable a supervisor may be, a person should continue trying to build a relationship with him or her. Bernie should indeed develop his horizontal relationships, but he still must work on his one vertical relationship. The author feels that no other good options were available for Bernie.

PROBLEM 5
Message

"Now you tell me . . ."

The author goes along with the decision to pass Jeff over for the supervisory position, for the following reasons.

1. It would be natural for Jeff's co-workers to resent him as a supervisor. He failed to build good horizontal working relationships with them when he had the chance. Productivity, under his leadership, could drop substantially.

2. An individual who doesn't learn how to build good horizontal relationships as an employee will probably have trouble building good vertical relationships as a supervisor. By neglecting

his horizontal working relationships when he first joined the department, Jeff made a classic human-relations mistake.

3. A supervisor achieves greater departmental productivity more from building good relationships than from the work he actually performs. Jeff would be a poor risk as a supervisor.

Jeff's supervisor should have worked with him to build good horizontal working relationships when Jeff first joined the firm. The supervisor, therefore, should assume some of the responsibility for not having prepared Jeff better for the promotional opportunity.

PROBLEM 6
Insight

"Okay, next time I'll cool it . . ."

Ted's impatience and exasperation are understandable. But the supervisor had a point and was right in counseling him to keep his cool and not further damage his horizontal relationships. Ted was well along the way to becoming a supervisor. If he had continued being critical of others he might have forfeited this opportunity.

It should be pointed out, however, that Ted was in a tough spot. It is extremely difficult to maintain personal productivity above your co-workers and still keep good relations with them. If Ted really wanted to be the next supervisor, this was the price he might have to pay.

The supervisor was wrong in not giving Ted the recognition he deserved sooner. He was also wrong in not counseling Ted before he became frustrated and damaged his horizontal relationships. Ted must learn, however, that few supervisors are perfect and that he must protect his future by being human-relations sensitive even when his supervisor is at fault.

PROBLEM 7
Choice

"I'm a Theory Y person myself."

You have a difficult choice. The older, Theory X supervisor might give you the following advantages: (1) he has been with the company longer and has had more experience, so he might be able to teach you more; and (2) although he may demand more from you, in the long run you might be a stronger person and eventually a better supervisor yourself because of it.

If you choose the younger, Theory Y supervisor, you might enjoy the following advantages: (1) you would probably become more involved under her leadership and, as a result, more productive; and (2) this supervisor would probably move up the management ladder sooner. If you work hard you might be able to take her place and move even higher later on because of her influence from above.

In answering the problem, consider the following:

1. In which work environment would you be most motivated and productive?

2. How would your personality and your values make it with each supervisor?

3. How ambitious are you to get into management?

If you fully understand the leadership styles of each of the two supervisors, you should be able to make the best decision. If you are adaptable, though, neither environment should hurt your personal progress.

PROBLEM 8
Communication

"Who needs other people?"

The case does not present Maria's side of the story. It is possible that Maria did not perceive that her unwillingness or inability to communicate freely was frustrating to her co-workers and supervisor. They wanted and needed to feel more relaxed around her. They needed a working relationship with her that was comfortable even though she may not have felt the same way about it.

Maria may also have failed to recognize that a lack of communication can lead to misinterpretation. She must learn two things: (1) two-way communication is absolutely essential for good, healthy working relationships, and (2) she may have been an excellent receiver, but she was apparently a poor sender.

How can the supervisor communicate this to her? There are three basic approaches. First, through a series of counseling sessions she can build a nonthreatening relationship where Maria can *learn* to communicate. To accomplish this Maria will gradually have to do more and more of the talking. During these sessions the supervisor should not break Maria's silent periods. She should refuse to communicate until Maria says something.

Second, the supervisor can ask for help from Maria's co-workers. She can ask them to help by being patient but persistent. Have them continue to ask her questions. Invite her to participate in coffee-break talks. Do anything to give her recognition, reinforcement, and confidence in her ability to communicate.

PROBLEM 9
Eagerness

"Me? Eager?"

It would be difficult to predict what kind of success pattern Ed might achieve. There are many dangers to his approach. How many dangers and how serious they might be depends on the kind of organization he joined, the management styles of his superiors, and the competitive environment within the corporate structure.

The overeager individual often moves so fast that he (or she) steps on other people's feelings without realizing it till much later. He often creates such a dynamic first impression that he cannot sustain it. He soon becomes known as a flash in the pan. In addition, the overzealous individual is not always well organized. As a result he hurts himself because he lacks the follow-through that establishes good permanent relationships and gets the job done to management's satisfaction.

Ed may have had to learn the hard way that the slower but smoother approach is often the smart way to get started. Steady progress is often the fastest way to the top. It should be said in defense of Ed, however, that there are some highly aggressive and fast-moving organizations where his approach would be less dangerous and perhaps even desired.

PROBLEM 10
Supervisor

"Supervisors can be difficult."

The author does not support any of the options listed. Numbers 1, 2, and 5 are really "cop-outs." Sandy would be running away from the problem. The other options all show Sandy's personal hostility and could lead to deeper problems. The author would suggest that Sandy initiate a conference with her supervisor to discuss the matter. She should act with the least possible emotional involvement.

If the supervisor makes some suggestions that would improve their relationship, Sandy would be wise to incorporate them into her behavior for an appropriate period of time. If this does not change things, Sandy might consider notifying the supervisor and going over his head with the problem. If, in time, neither step works, Sandy should request a transfer.

Many additional facts are needed in the case. Has the supervisor had a pattern of poor relationships with new employees? Are there any serious psychological problems involved? Has Sandy, because of possible hostility, been provoking the situation? What about Sandy's productivity and horizontal relationships?

Although the supervisor has the larger share of responsibility in creating and maintaining a good vertical relationship, Sandy also has a responsibility. Her problem might be more serious if she had been with the firm three years instead of three months. She would have a bigger time investment. But the stakes are still very high, especially when one considers that she was unemployed for a year. Sandy needs to start building a successful job pattern for herself.

PROBLEM 11
Confrontation

"A person's attitude can stand just so much."

Jane did the right thing under the circumstances. After two months she had had sufficient time to discover that the cause of Ms. Robertson's critical attitude was deep-seated and that time alone would probably not solve the problem. Jane took time to investigate and gather some facts. She discovered, among other things, that two former employees in her position resigned because of Ms. Robertson and her attitude. In other words this was not surface teasing or testing.

Although Jane took a serious human-relations risk by standing up to Ms. Robertson, she had at least a fair chance of resolving the problem and helping her future. If successful, everybody would come out ahead, including the company and Ms. Robertson.

The reader may not fully agree with the *way* Jane approached Ms. Robertson or the way in which she expressed herself. To some it may appear that she was too direct and forceful. To others she may have appeared to be overly apologetic. Everyone must go about confrontations of this nature in her (or his) own individual manner. But the principle remains that the cards must often be laid on the table if a sound working relationship is to be created or restored.

PROBLEM 12
Habits

"As bad as that . . . ?"

Gary quickly created an extremely difficult situation for himself. He damaged his personal reputation as a management trainee among a number of key management people. He also seriously hurt his horizontal relations with his co-workers. The damage was so serious that Gary might have to look elsewhere for a fresh start.

Although it took only three months for Gary to create this situation, repairing his damaged reputation could be slowgoing and quite difficult. It takes time to live down a bad reputation. It also takes patience. And in Gary's case, it would take a whole new set of habits.

Should he try?

It would depend upon whether or not Gary can find another company that would equal his present one. Can he locate another job as a management trainee in the kind of organization he wants? Is it in the geographical area he wants? Does it have all the advantages and benefits of his present company?

If so, Gary should start over. If not, he should do two things: (1) strongly discipline himself as far as being absent or late was concerned, so that no further damage would be done; and (2) make a special effort to rebuild the relationships he previously injured. Gary's personal progress would depend heavily upon the success he achieved.

PROBLEM 13
Listening

"Good listeners are hard to find."

It is easy to understand the supervisor's impatience with Fay's apparent inability to receive verbal messages. However, it is doubtful whether his threat to terminate her unless she did an about-face in two weeks was justified. In the first place, Fay is a very sensitive and emotional person. Such an insensitive approach to the problem was bound to cause her to react in a highly emotional manner, thus compounding the problem.

In the second place, the supervisor should have quietly counseled her once or twice along the way and made a few specific suggestions that might have helped. There is no doubt that the organization could profit from Fay's talent. More effort should have been made to resolve the matter.

There are a number of things that Fay could have done to overcome the problem and perhaps save her job: (1) she could have played it safe and had her hearing checked; (2) she could have concentrated on putting her creative mind out of gear while she was listening to the supervisor's words; (3) she could have taken notes while the supervisor was talking, to back up the verbal message; (4) she could have asked his permission to bring back preliminary sketches before proceeding; and (5) immediately after each verbal communications session, she could have taken some time to think over carefully what had been said before moving ahead with the artwork.

PROBLEM 14
Dilemma

"Me? Fall for a rumor?"

Sylvia made two mistakes. First, she accepted as fact a comment that was not authenticated and could easily have been a rumor. Her second mistake, however, was more serious than the first: she permitted the possible rumor to disturb her emotionally to the point where it noticeably hurt her productivity.

The facts were not presented in the case, but it is quite possible that the real reason Mr. Young was made department head instead of Sylvia was because Sylvia's efficiency on the job dropped to the level where management decided to pass her over. If this was what happened, Sylvia permitted a simple rumor to do the greatest possible damage to her future.

PROBLEM 15
Preference

"What's in it for me?"

Angelo had an intriguing but difficult decision ahead of him. In making it he should have taken a long look at himself. Where would his personality have fit in best? How important was immediate monetary success versus long-range security to him? What were his long-term goals? If Angelo became impatient and frustrated over slow but steady progress, he should have thought twice about joining a company with a firm PFW policy. The zigzag route to the top might be better.

On the other hand, if Angelo was willing and able to adjust to the longer, slower route, company B is his best bet. They could provide more and better training, would perhaps encourage him to finish college at night at their expense, and might keep better track of him.

If Angelo sought more immediate success, and he was willing to take the risks involved, company A would have been his best bet. They might have pushed more responsibility his way sooner. They might also have been less stifling and have expected less conformity.

He should have kept in mind, however, that he might have had to train himself more. The inside competition might have been more aggressive. He might not have been given much time to prepare for additional responsibility. There is also the possibility that he might have found it advisable to move from one company to another to make it to the top.

There are many hidden factors involved in such a decision. Angelo should have weighed each one carefully. He would also have been wise to talk it over with his wife, since her happiness was also important to his decision.

PROBLEM 16
Plateau

"Plateaus take forever."

It is doubtful that the plateau can be eliminated entirely. The following might help: (1) cut back on the employment of management trainees so that there is less of a logjam; (2) train more non-four-year college graduates for junior-management roles because they might be willing to stay there longer; and (3) reconstitute the roles so that the line between junior and middle management is less distinguishable and movement between the two levels is easier.

Help junior-management people survive the plateau. Give them greater recognition as they approach the plateau period. This could include new job titles and modest pay increases. Counsel them on long-term goals. In other words, show them why it is worth waiting. Design special in-house training programs to prepare them for mid-management responsibilities. Assign more responsibilities to lower roles to provide continuing learning opportunities. Involve both levels of management in a series of seminars to find a solution to the problem.

PROBLEM 17
Options

"I hate decision making."

The author would support the first four options. The remaining six offer very little. Some, in fact, could do more harm than good.

Norman works for a company that has many advantages. He might not improve his situation elsewhere. His first step, therefore, is to motivate himself. If his attitude improves, he will be more likely to be considered for a better role. Norman should then talk with his supervisor about assuming more responsibility. He might get some assistance, perhaps psychological support, from a discussion with the right person.

When an employee becomes dissatisfied or reaches a plateau it is always a good idea to search for another role with another company. There are two reasons for this: (1) the individual can thus find out whether or not he (or she) can really improve himself—instead of just thinking about it—and (2) searching for a better role often motivates the person in his present job because it helps him get out of a mental rut. It can also make him see more clearly the advantages (or disadvantages) of his present job.

PROBLEM 18
Frustration

"Me and my big mouth!"

The company was at fault for not having better communication with Vic regarding his future role. Even so, it would be difficult to justify such an outburst in a man with his education and experience.

What could Vic have done to prevent it? If he had been sufficiently aware of his building inner tensions, he might have been able to release them off the job—by working in his yard, playing golf, or taking part in some other physical activity that would better suit his style.

It is doubtful whether Vic had seriously hurt his career at this point. This, of course, depended on the personnel officer who was on the receiving end of the outburst. If he was aware of the frustration-aggression idea, he could have easily appreciated Vic's behavior and not made a negative judgment against him.

However, the personnel director could have interpreted Vic's outbust as unstable or immature behavior.

To play it safe Vic should have done everything possible to strengthen his relationship with the personnel officer. If he felt an apology was in order, he should have offered it. He would have benefited from his experience substantially if it taught him to watch for inner signals of tension. That way, he could divert any aggressive behavior into less harmful channels.

PROBLEM 19
Hostility

"Better late than never."

It is possible that Lupe transmitted her hostility to her superiors and co-workers in such a way as to injure relationships. In other words, her attitude may have been showing in a negative and disturbing manner. First, she could have built better relationships with her co-workers by spending more time with them and by being more concerned with their problems. Second, she should have set out to prove that she was editorial material by doing superior work in her field. That way she might be given opportunities to participate in some of the more exciting assignments. Griping about her present routine assignments would not accomplish this. Lupe should have helped the editors in such a way that they would go to bat with management to make her an editor.

PROBLEM 20
Interview

"I'm ready for a fresh start."

The author would accept the following answers as "models."

1. "In doing my pre-interview investigation, I discovered that your organization has a strong promotion-from-within policy. I also found that you have an ambitious expansion program for the next five years, and that you have an excellent reputation in the

industry for treating people fairly. These features appeal to me very much."

2. "I feel I can contribute a great deal over the long run because I am willing to listen, learn, and develop my leadership style. I would bring many skills into the company and I would develop many more. My goal would be to reach an important management role where my influence in building a stronger company would be felt."

3. "I believe I have developed many human-relations skills. I can not only build good relations with co-workers and superiors, but I can also maintain them. I am good at problem solving, I am sensitive to the needs of others, and I understand the positive relationship between high productivity and good human relations."

4. "I reached a plateau in my present company two years ago. Since then I have not been able to take a significant step upward. I believe the main reason is that the company is in a period of reorganization and retraction. However, because I was young when I joined them, I too made some mistakes. I have learned a great deal since then and I think I am ready to take full advantage of a fresh start."